RECORDED VERSIONS GUITAR

AUTHENTIC TRANSCRIPTIONS WITH NOTES AND TABLATURE

R&B GUITAR

D1594887

ISBN 0-7935-8282-2

HAL•LEONARD® CORPORATION

7777 W. BLUEMOUND RD. P.O. BOX 13819 MILWAUKEE, WI 53213

Visit Hal Leonard Online at
www.halleonard.com

Brick House

Words and Music by Lionel Richie, Ronald La Pread, Walter Orange, Milan Williams, Thomas McClary and William King

*Key signature denotes A Dorian.

**Tap body of gtr. near pickup w/ pick.

(cont. in notation)

*Chord symbols reflect tonality of gtr. 1

Verse

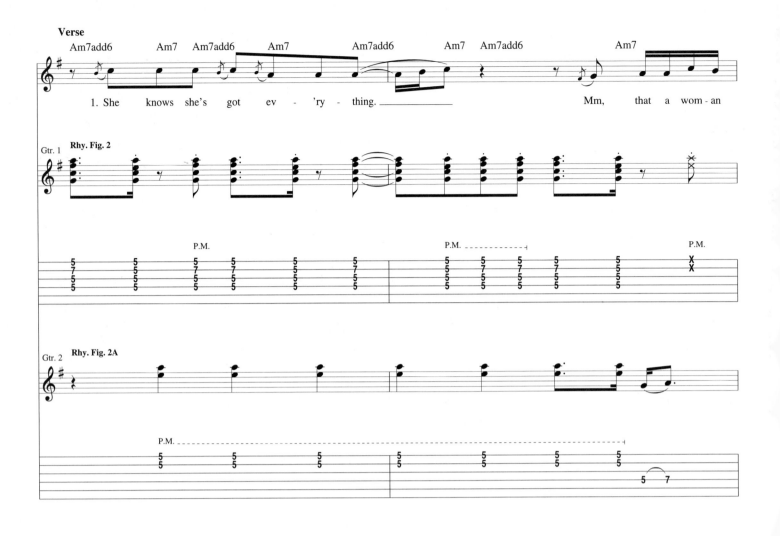

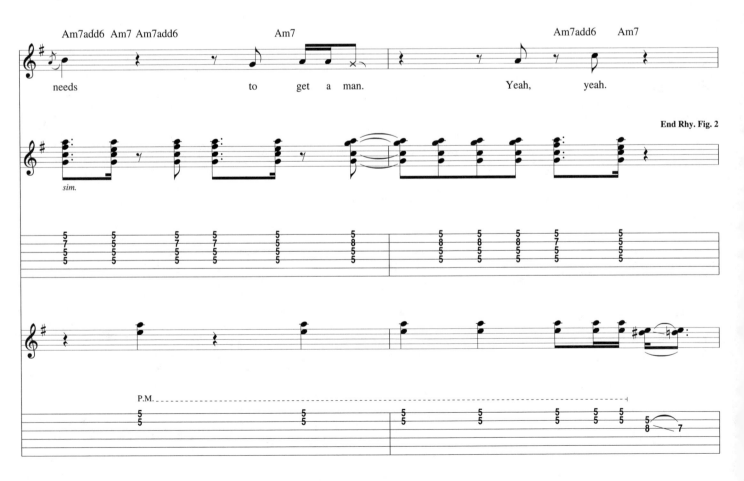

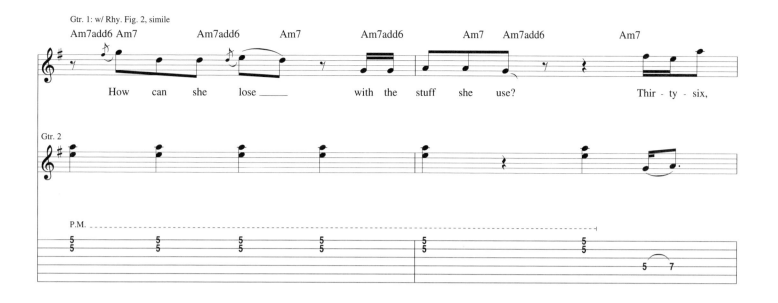

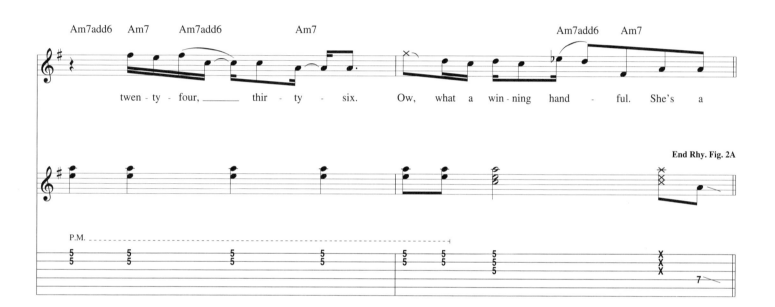

Chorus

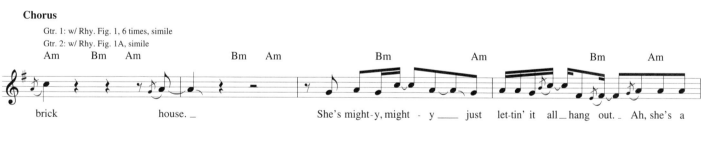

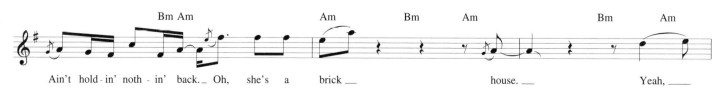

Bridge

Am11

Gtr. 1

A shake it down, shake it down now. ___

A shake it down, shake it down now. __

Gtr. 2

1.

___ A shake it down, shake it down now. __

A shake it down, shake it down, down, down. __

2.

A shake it down say, "Ow."

sim.

Chorus

Gtr. 1: w/ Rhy. Fig. 1, 4 times, simile
Gtr. 2: w/ Rhy. Fig. 1A, 1st 3 meas., simile

Am   Bm   Am   Bm   Am   Bm   Am

Brick   house. ___   Yeah,   she's   might - y, might - y _____   a just

Gtr. 2: w/ Rhy. Fill 1   Gtr. 2: w/ Rhy. Fig. 1A, 1st 4 meas., simile

Bm   Am   Am   Bm   Am   Bm   Am   Bm   Am

let-tin' it all __ hang out. __ Ow,   a brick   house. __   Yeah   she's the one, __ the on - ly one __

Bridge

Gtr. 1: w/ Rhy. Fig. 1, 2 times, simile
Gtr. 2: w/ Rhy. Fig. 1A, 1st 4 meas., simile

Bm   Am   Am   Bm   Am

built   like an Am - a - zon. __   Yeah. __   Shake it down, shake it down, shake it now,   now. __

Bm   Am   Bm   Am

___ Shake it down, shake it down, shake it now,   now. __   Shake it down, shake it down, shake it now,   now. __

1.

Bm   Am

___ Shake it down, shake it down, shake it, shake it.

2.

Bm   Am

Shake it down, shake it down.   Shake it.

7

Interlude

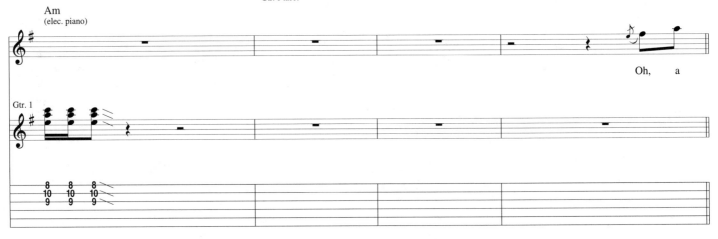

Outro

*Chord symbols reflect implied tonality.

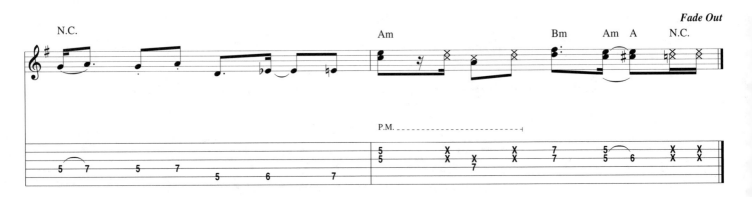

But It's Alright

Words and Music by Jerome L. Jackson and Pierre Tubbs

Xylophone Solo

*Xylophone arr. for gtr.

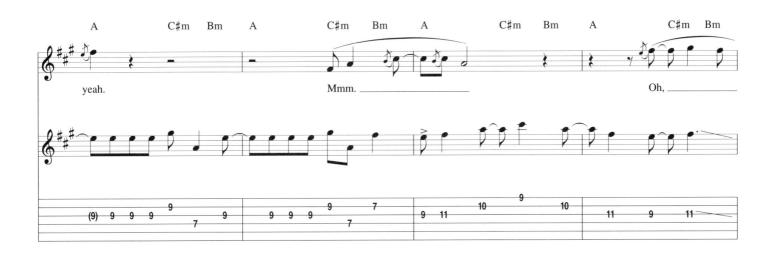

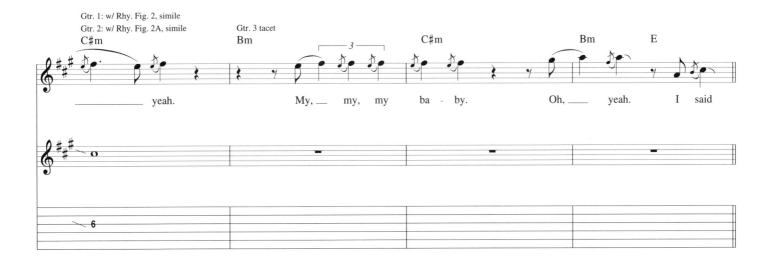

Chorus

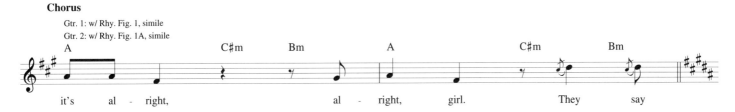

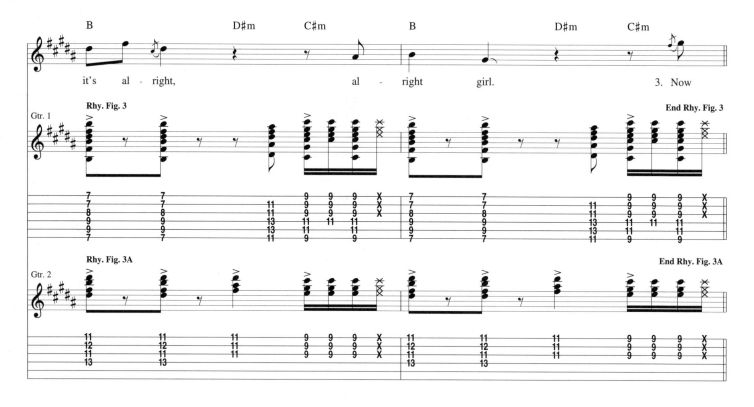

it's al - right, al - right girl. 3. Now

Verse

Gtr. 1: w/ Rhy. Fig. 3, 4 times, simile
Gtr. 2: w/ Rhy. Fig.3A, 4 times, simile

there's one thing I wan - na say. You'll meet a guy who'll make you pay. He'll

treat ya bad, he'll make you sad and you will ru - in the love you had. Oh, but I

hate to say I told you so, but,

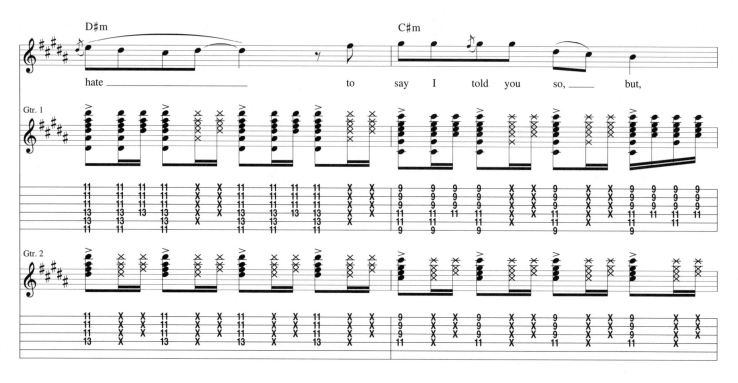

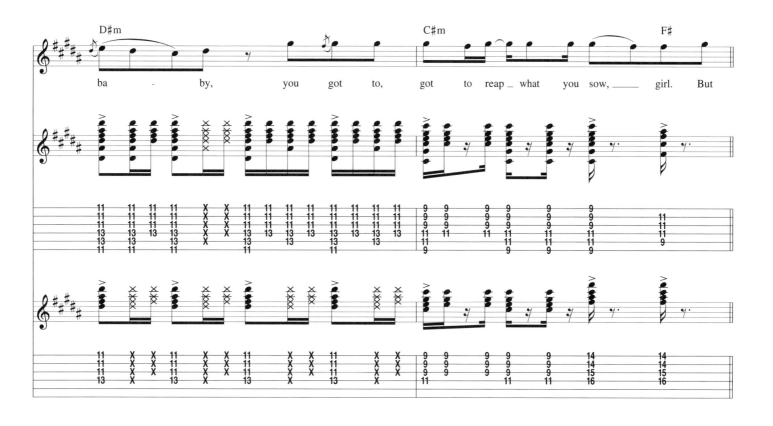

ba - by, you got to, got to reap what you sow, _____ girl. But

Chorus

Gtr. 1: w/ Rhy. Fig. 3, 2 times, simile
Gtr. 2: w/ Rhy. Fig. 3A, 2 times, simile

it's al - right, al - right, girl. You are

Verse

Gtr. 1: w/ Rhy. Fig. 3, till fade, simile
Gtr. 2: w/ Rhy. Fig. 3A, till fade, simile

pay - ing now, but, it's al - right. 4. So good - bye now, good -

bye, girl. You're pay - ing now, so, bye - bye. You

Begin Fade

hurt me once, _____ you hurt me twice, oh, _____ but a, ba - by, _____ don't

Fade Out

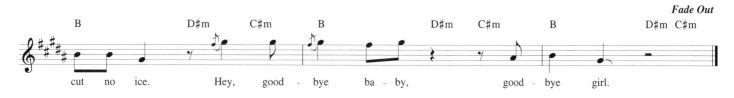

cut no ice. Hey, good - bye ba - by, good - bye girl.

For Once in My Life

Words by Ronald Miller Music by Orlando Murden

Verse

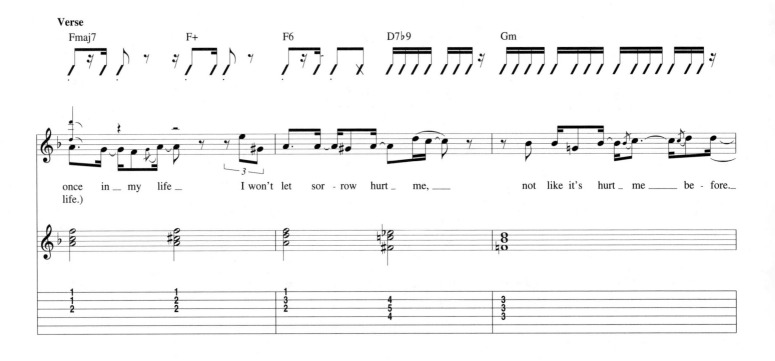

once in my life ___ I won't let sor - row hurt _ me, ___ not like it's hurt _ me ___ be - fore. ___
life.)

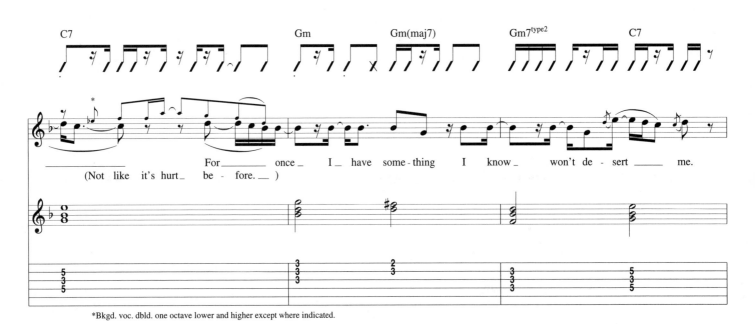

___ For ___ once _ I _ have some - thing I know _ won't de - sert ___ me.
(Not like it's hurt _ be - fore. ___)

*Bkgd. voc. dbld. one octave lower and higher except where indicated.

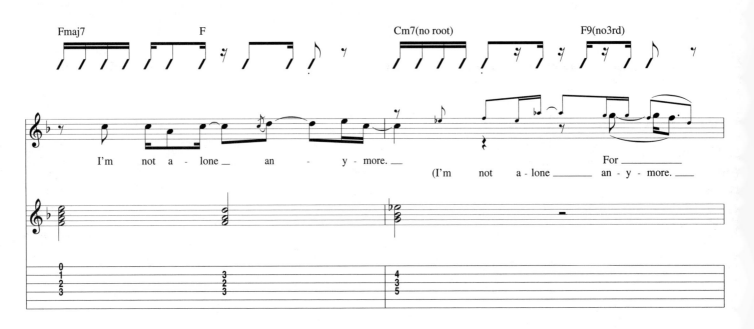

I'm not a - lone ___ an - y - more. ___ (I'm not a - lone ___ an - y - more. ___ For ___

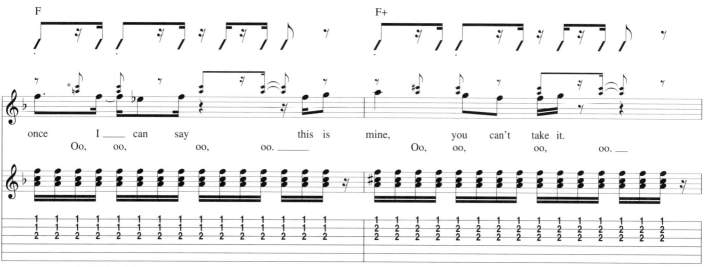

once I ___ can say   this is   mine,   you can't   take it.
Oo,   oo,   oo,   oo. ___   Oo, oo,   oo,   oo. ___

*not dbld., next 4 meas.

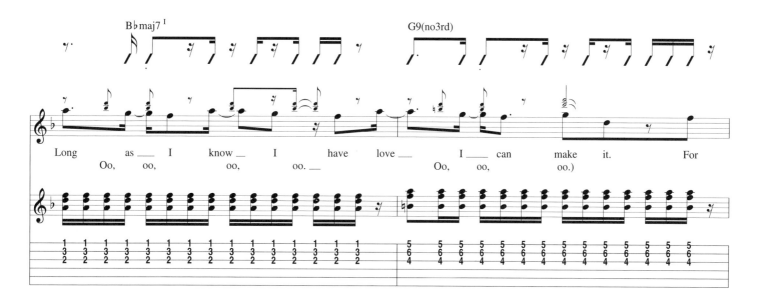

Long   as ___ I know ___ I   have   love ___ I ___ can   make   it.   For
Oo,   oo,   oo,   oo. ___   Oo,   oo,   oo.)

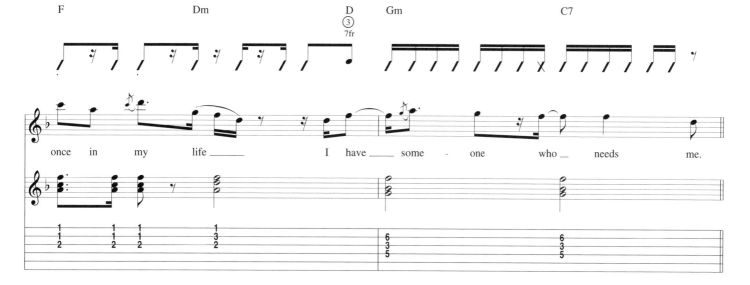

once in   my   life _____   I have ___ some - one   who ___ needs   me.

Interlude

Gtrs. 1 & 2 tacet

w/ Lead Voc. ad lib.

(Some - one   who   needs   me. ___   Some - one   who   needs   me. _____)

**Chord symbols reflect overall tonality.

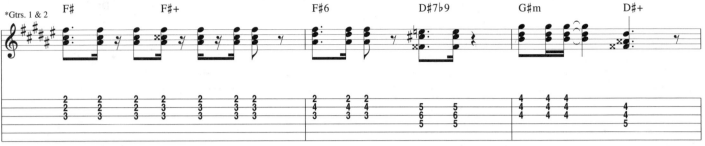

*composite arrangement

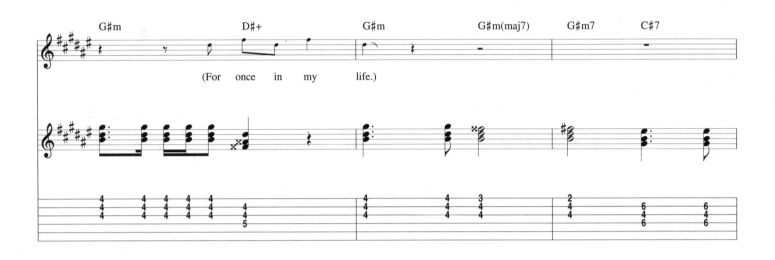

(For once in my life.)

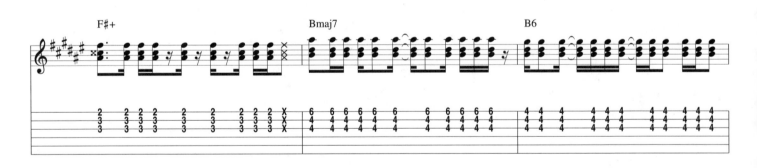

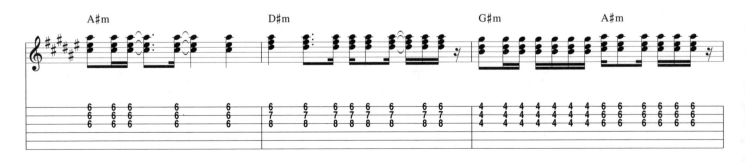

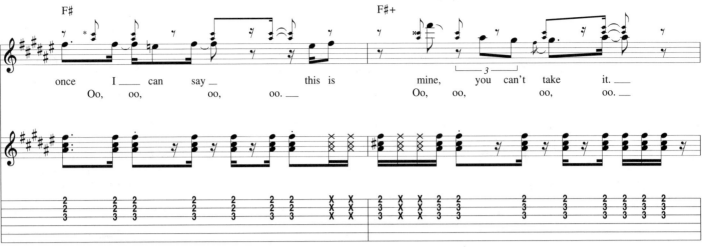

*not dbld., next 4 meas.

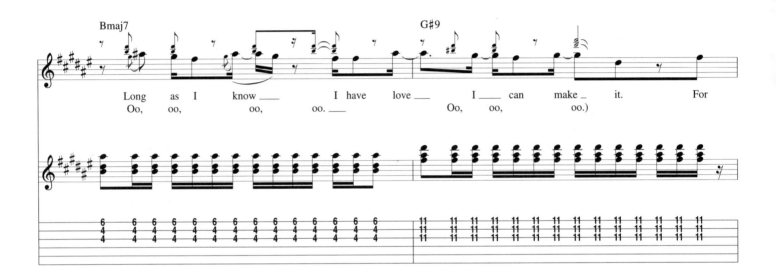

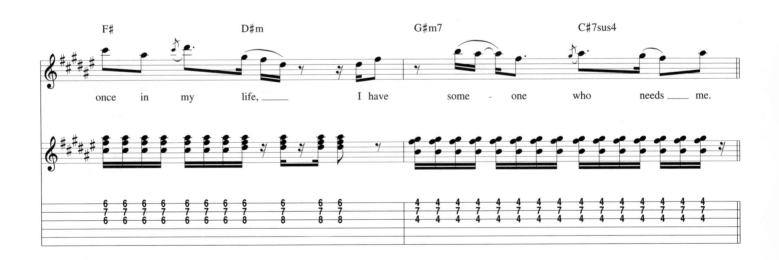

Play 3 Times and Fade

Outro

Gtrs. 1 & 2 tacet
w/ Lead Voc. ad lib., till fade

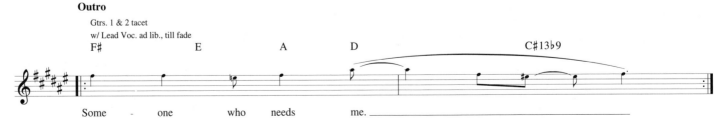

I Can't Help Myself
(Sugar Pie, Honey Bunch)

Words and Music by Brian Holland, Lamont Dozier and Edward Holland

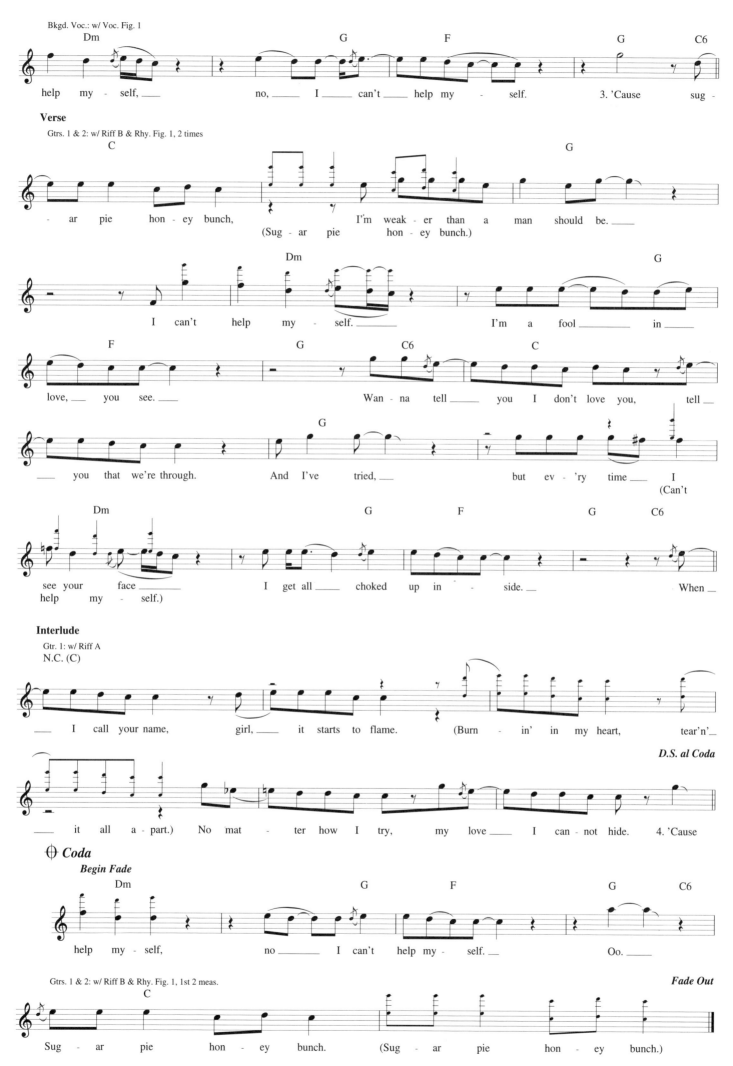

I Got the Feelin'

Words and Music by James Brown

Chorus

Gtr. 1: w/ Rhy. Fig. 1, 2 times
Gtr. 2: w/ Rhy. Fig. 2, 1 1/2 times

Gtr. 2: w/ Rhy. Fill 1

Good God!
Ba - by!

I _____ got the feel - in', uh.
I got the feel - in', ba - by, can't help it.

Al - right.

Ba - by, ba - by, ba - by,

ba - by, ba - by, ba - by,   ba - by, ba - by, ba - by,   ba - by, ba - by.   2. I got the
I'm on a

Verse

Gtr. 1: w/ Rhy. Fig. 1, 7 times
Gtr. 2: w/ Rhy. Fig. 2, 7 times

feel - in', ba - by.   Ba - by.

Some - times I'm up,   some - times I'm down. _____   My

heart, _____   al - right, _____ I'm a, real - ly down, _____ a lev - el with

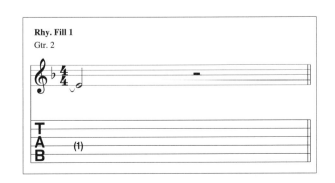

Rhy. Fill 1
Gtr. 2

I Heard It Through the Grapevine

Words and Music by Norman J. Whitfield and Barrett Strong

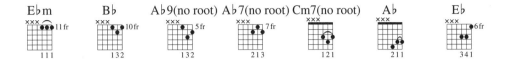

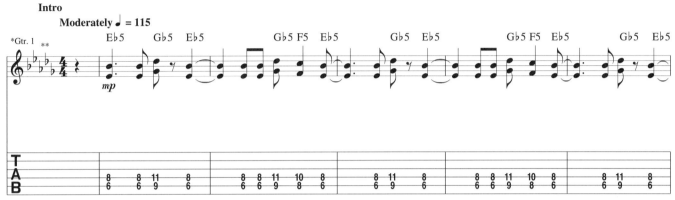

*Kybd. arr. for gtr.

**Key Signature denotes Eb Dorian

Coda
Outro

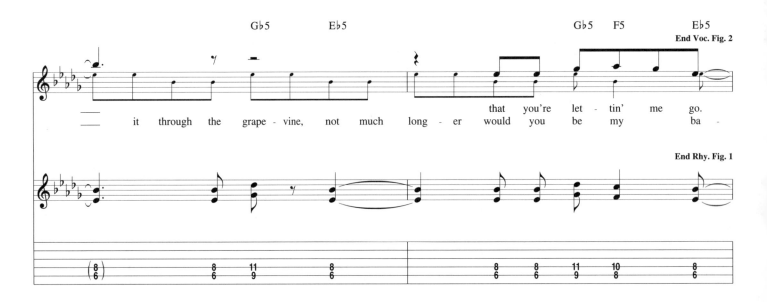

Bkgd. Voc.: w/ Voc. Fig. 2, 1 1/2 times
Gtr. 1: w/ Rhy. Fig. 1, 1 1/2 times

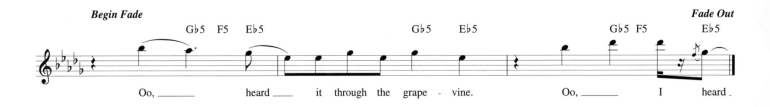

Additional Lyrics

2. I know a man ain't supposed to cry,
   But these tears, I can't hold inside.
   Losing you would end my life, you see.
   'Cause you mean that much to me.
   You could've told me yourself that you love someone else.
   Instead, I heard...

3. People say believe half of what you see.
   Some and none of what you hear.
   But I can't help from being confused.
   If it's true, please tell me dear.
   Do you plan to let me go for the other guy you loved before?

I Just Want to Celebrate

Words and Music by Nick Zesses and Dino Fekaris

%> Chorus

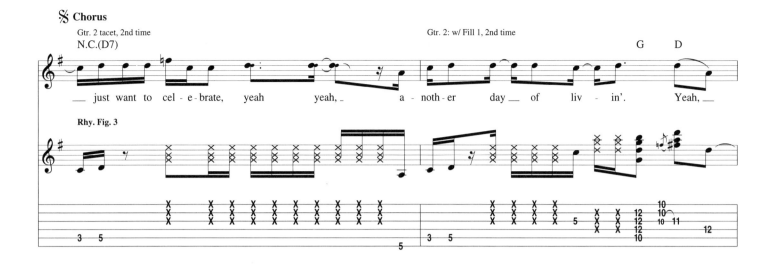

Bridge

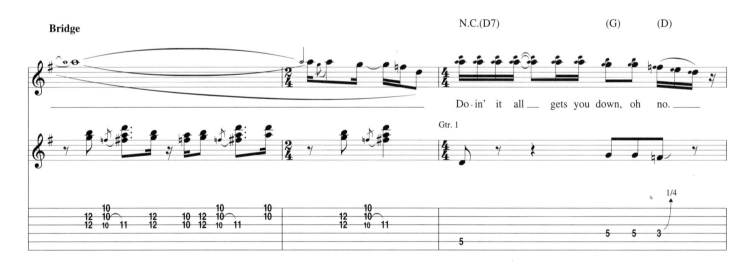

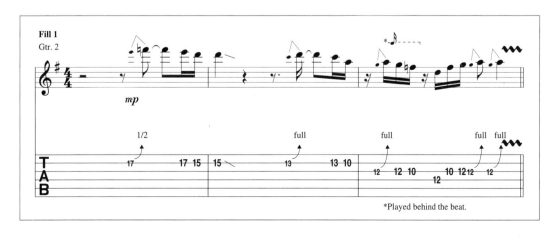

*Played behind the beat.

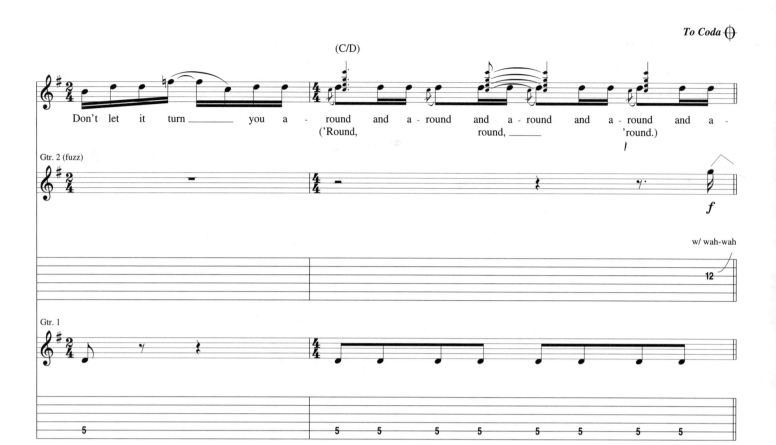

I Second That Emotion

Words and Music by William "Smokey" Robinson and Alfred Cleveland

1. May - be you wan-na give_ me kis-ses sweet, _____ but

on - ly for one night ____ with no re - peat. ____ And

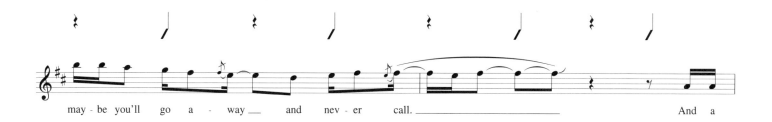

may-be you'll go a - way ___ and nev - er call. _____ And a

Bridge

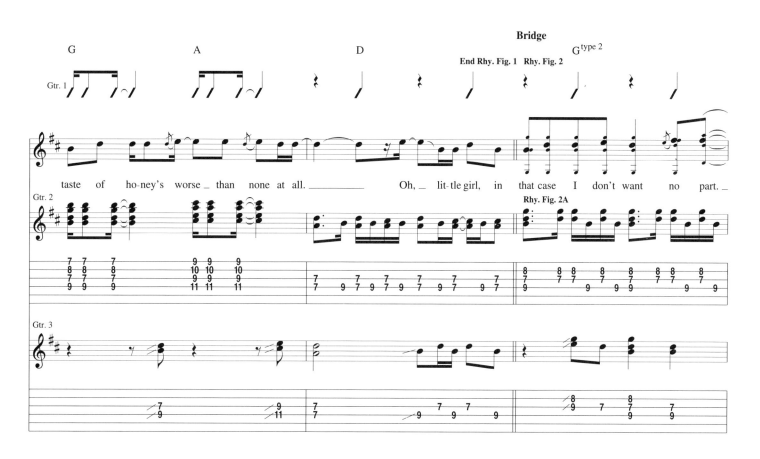

taste of ho-ney's worse _ than none at all. _____ Oh, _ lit-tle girl, in that case I don't want no part. _

I do be - lieve that that would on - ly break my heart. _____ Oh, ___ but

Bkgd. Voc.: w/ Voc. Fig. 2

Gtr. 2: w/ Rhy. Fig. 3A
Gtr. 3: w/ Riff B

if you feel like giv - in' me _____ a life - time of de - vo - tion _____

_____ I sec - ond that e - mo - tion. Oh, 2. May -

Verse

Gtr. 1: w/ Rhy. Fig. 1
Gtr. 2: w/ Rhy. Fig. 1A, 3 times, simile
Gtr. 3: w/ Riff A, 3 times, simile
Bkgd. Voc.: w/ Voc. Fig. 3

- be you think that love would tie you down _____ and you don't have _ the time _ to hang a - round. _

Voc. Fig. 2

Oo. _____

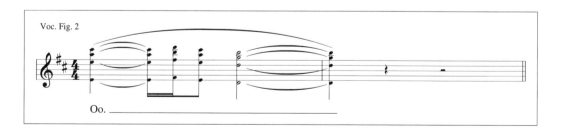

Voc. Fig. 3

Oo. _____ Doo, doo, _ doo, doo, doo _____

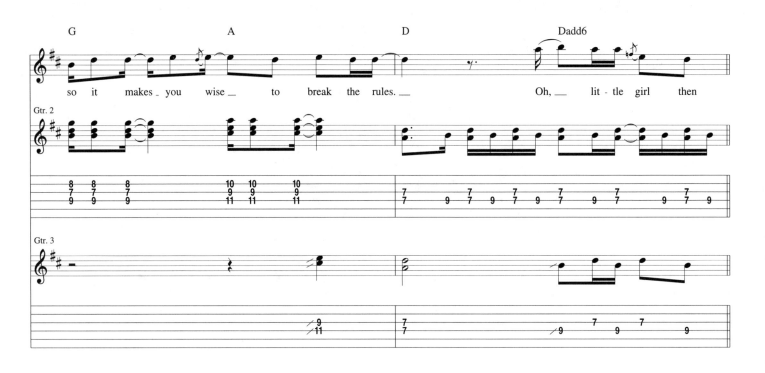

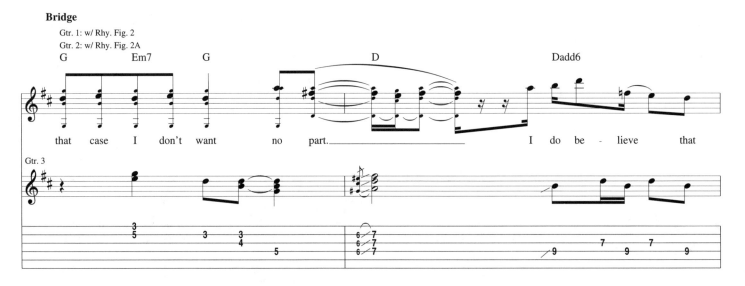

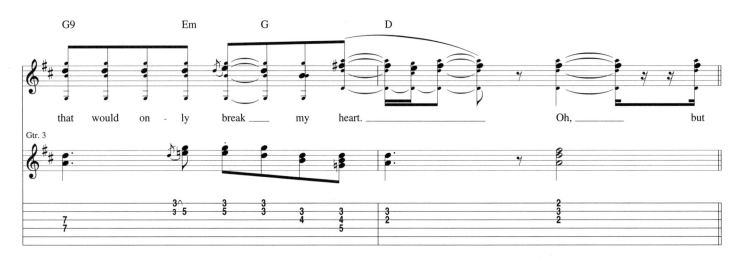

Chorus

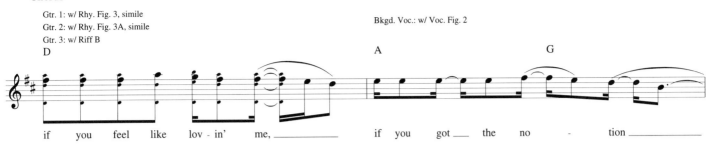

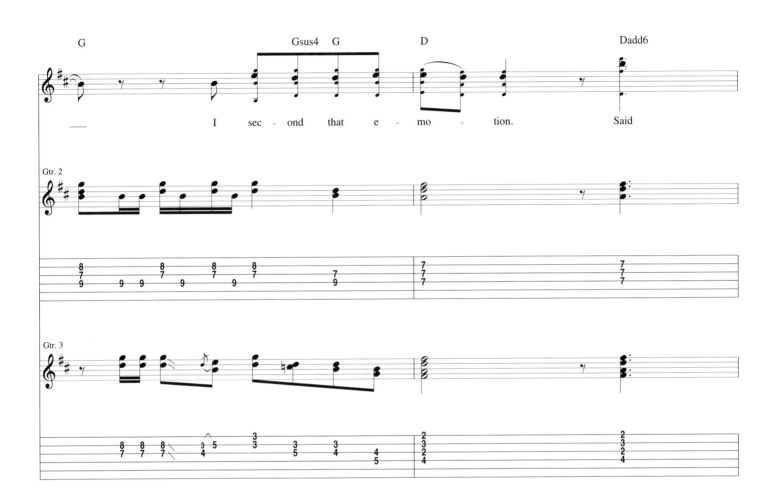

— uh, I sec - ond that e - mo - tion. Oh, oh.

Interlude

Oh, oh.

Bridge

Gtr. 1: w/ Rhy. Fig. 2
Gtr. 2: w/ Rhy. Fig. 2A

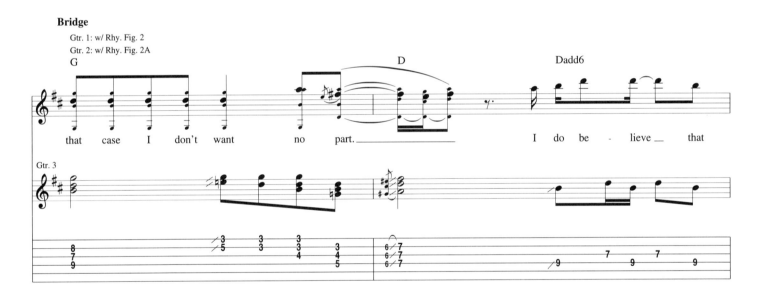

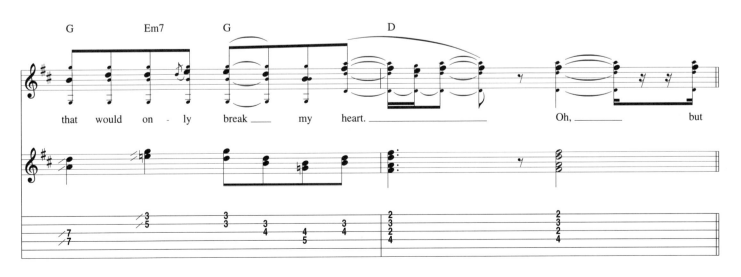

Chorus

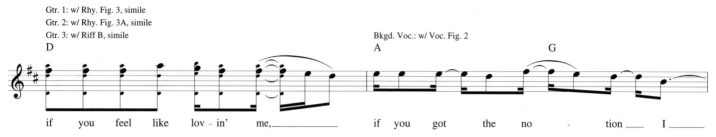

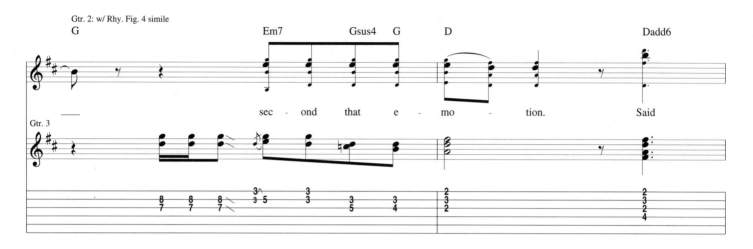

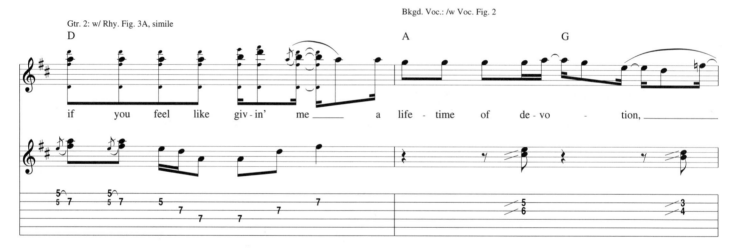

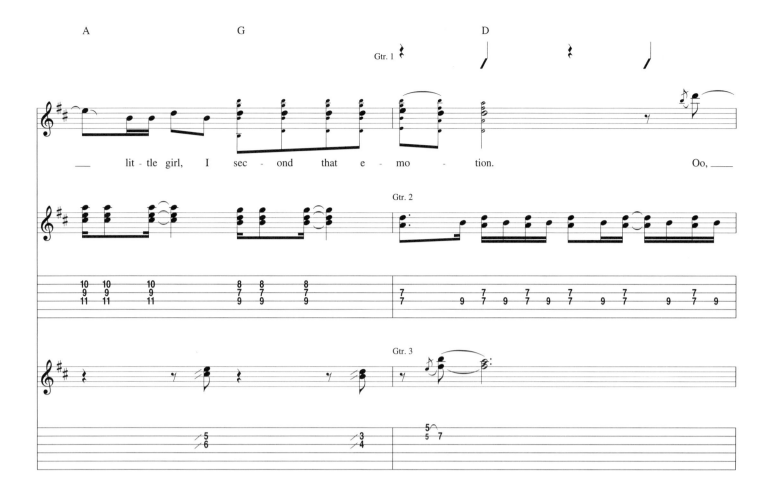

lit - tle girl, I sec - ond that e - mo - tion. Oo, _____

Begin Fade   *Fade Out*

_____ lit - tle girl, I sec - ond that e - mo - tion.

45

It's Your Thing

By Rudolph Isley, Ronald Isley and O'Kelly Isley

My Girl

Words and Music by William "Smokey" Robinson and Ronald White

Chorus

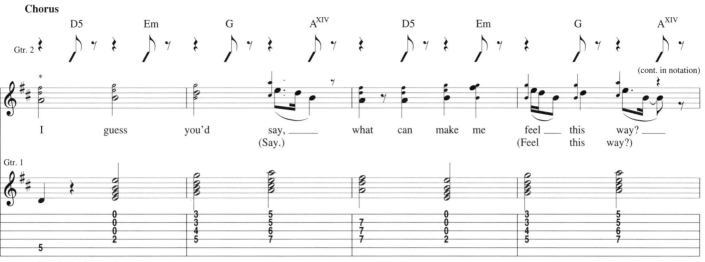

*Bkgd. Voc. low in mix

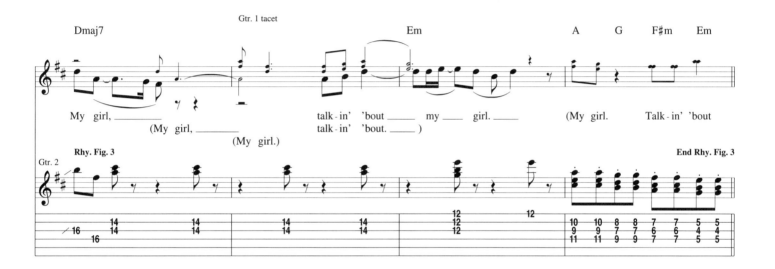

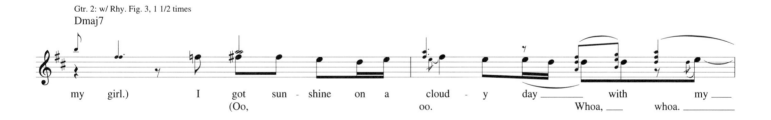

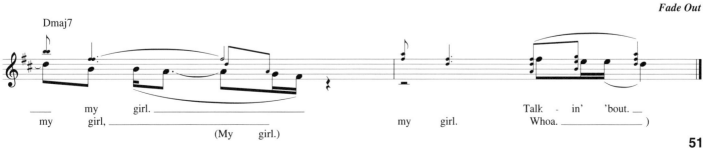

Papa Was a Rollin' Stone

Words and Music by Norman Whitfield and Barrett Strong

* Key signature denotes Bb Dorian

** Includes Gtrs. 2 & 3

* + = closed (toe down) o = open (toe up)

Verse

ber. That day I'll al-ways re-mem – ber, yes I will, 'cause

that was the day ___ that my dad - dy died, ___

I nev - er got a chance ___ to see ___ him. Nev -

er heard ___ noth-in' but bad ___ things a - bout him. Ma - ma, I'm de - pend - ing on you ___

53

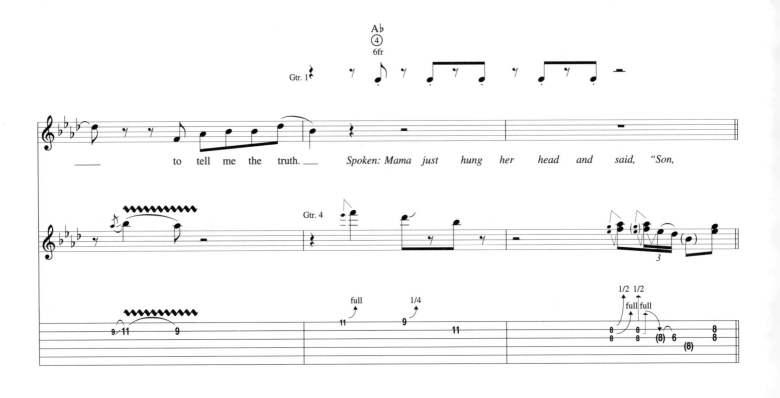

Chorus

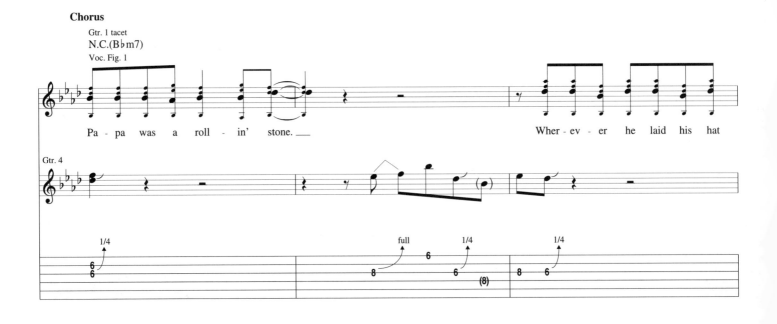

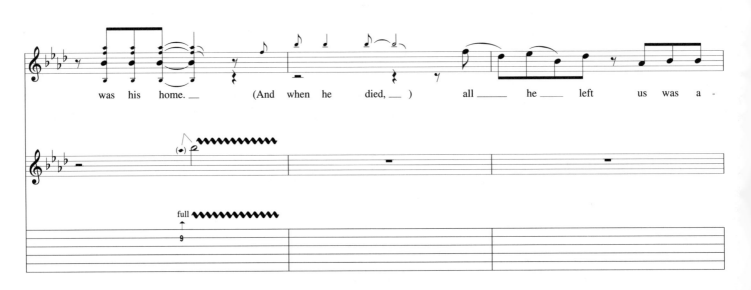

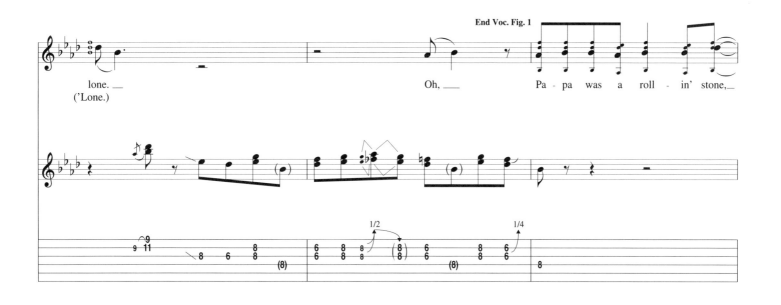

lone. ___
('Lone.)

Oh, ___ Pa - pa was a roll - in' stone, ___

___ my ___ son, ___ yeah.

Wher - ev - er he laid his hat was his home. ___ (And

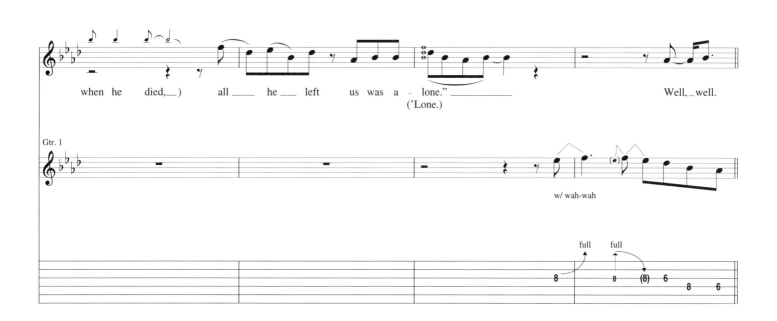

when he died,__) all ___ he ___ left ___ us was a - lone." _____
('Lone.)

Well, _well.

Trumpet Solo

Interlude

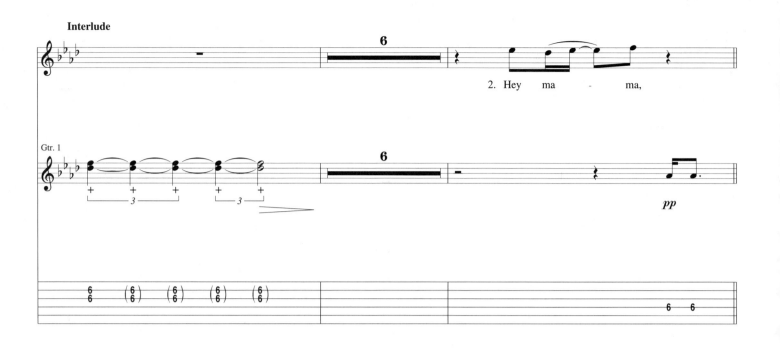

2. Hey ma - ma,

Verse

is it true   what they say,   that   Pa - pa nev - er worked a day   in   his   life?

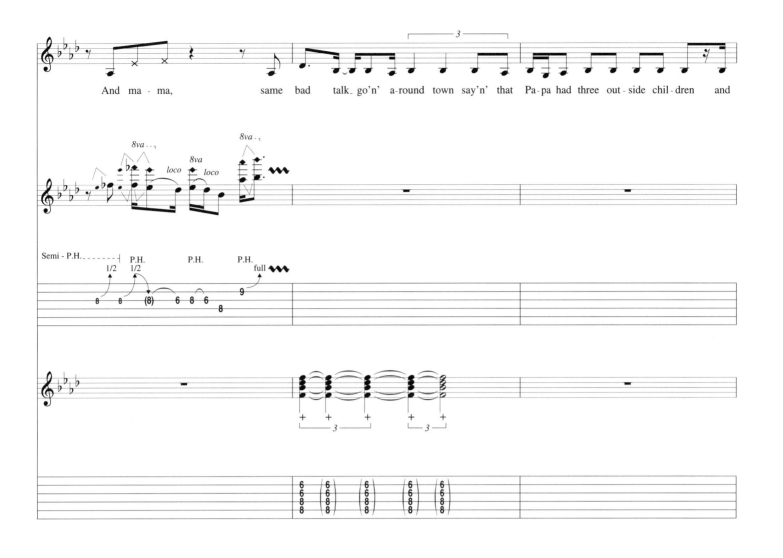

some store - front preach - in', talk - in' a - bout sav - in' souls,_ and all _ the time _ leach - in'. Deal -

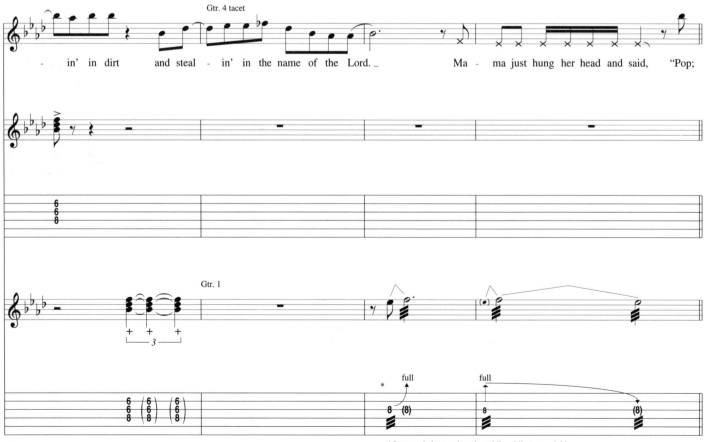

- in' in dirt and steal - in' in the name of the Lord. _ Ma - ma just hung her head and said, "Pop;

*Open and close wah-wah rapidly while trem. picking

𝄋 Chorus

Gtr. 3: w/ Fill 1, 2nd time; w/ Rhy. Fig. 3, 4 times, simile, 3rd time
Gtr. 4: w/ Riff B, 8 times
Bkgd. Voc.: w/ Voc. Fig. 1, 2 times

Pa - pa was a roll - in' stone, _____ my son. _____

Wher - ev - er he laid his hat was his home. _____ And

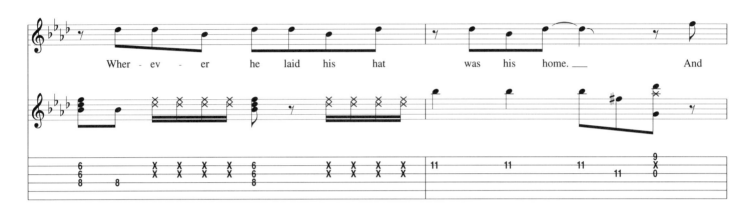

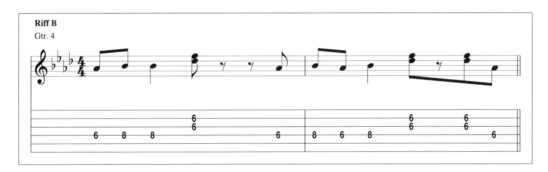

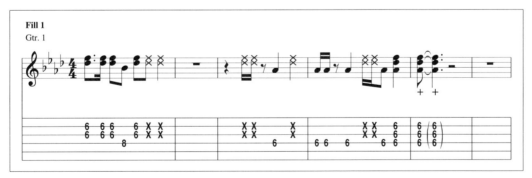

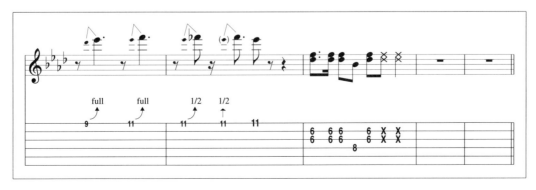

59

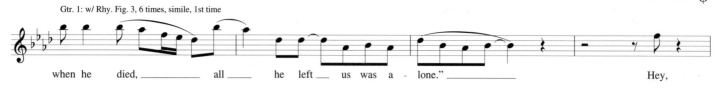

when he died, _____ all ____ he left ____ us was a - lone." _____ Hey,

Pa - pa was a roll - in' stone. ____ Dat gone it. Wher - ev - er he laid his hat was his home. _____ And

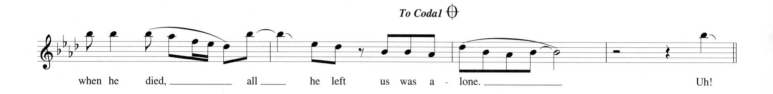

when he died, _____ _____ all ____ he left us was a - lone. _____ Uh!

Trumpet Solo
B♭m

Gtr. 1

(cont. in notation)

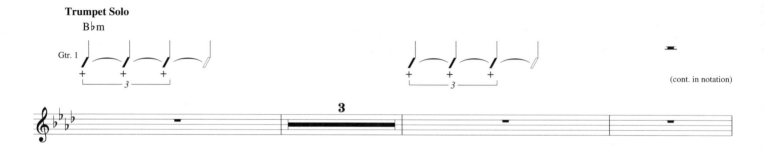

Interlude
B♭m

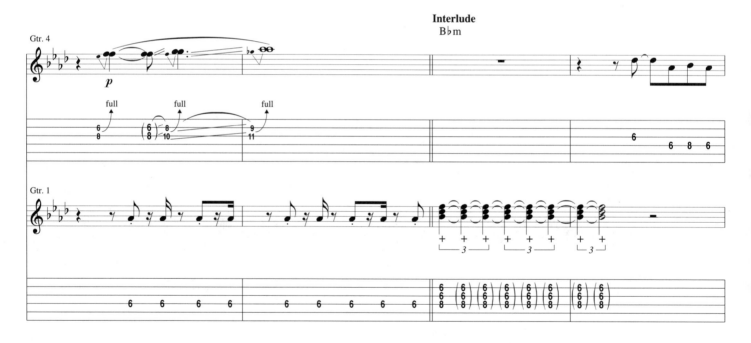

Fill 2
Gtr. 1

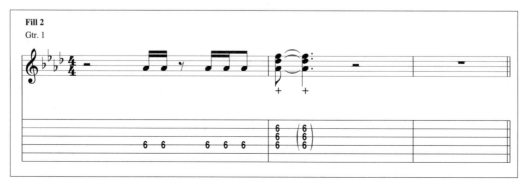

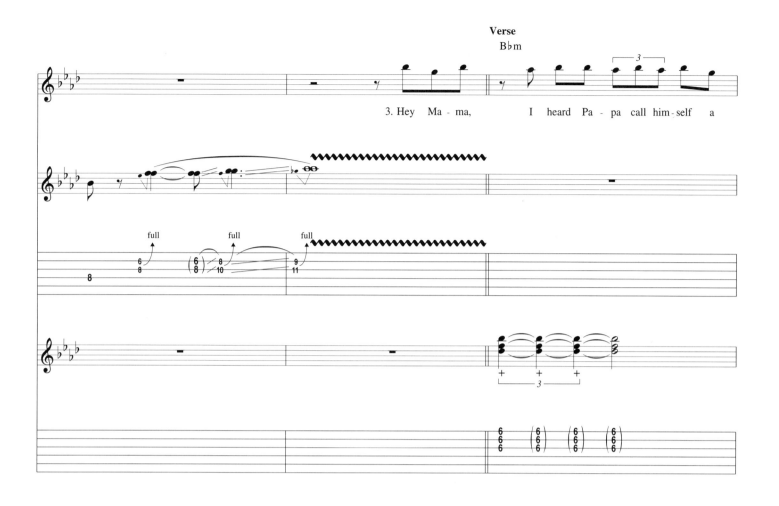

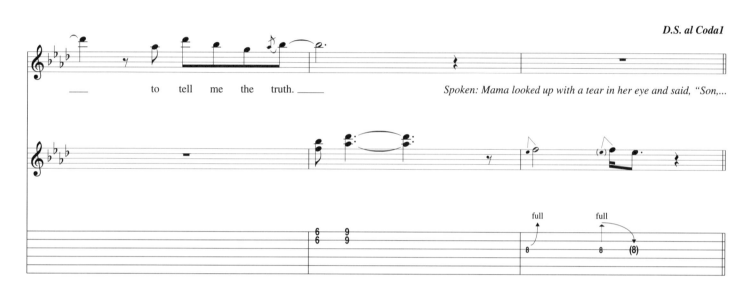

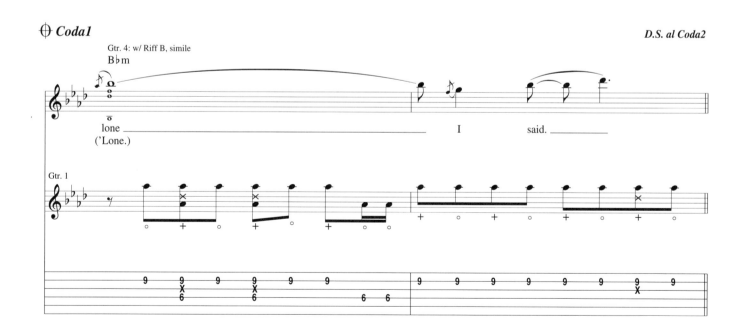

Papa's Got a Brand New Bag

Words and Music by James Brown

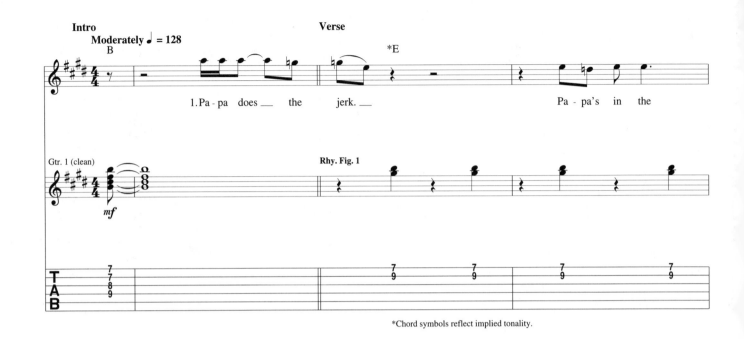

*Chord symbols reflect implied tonality.

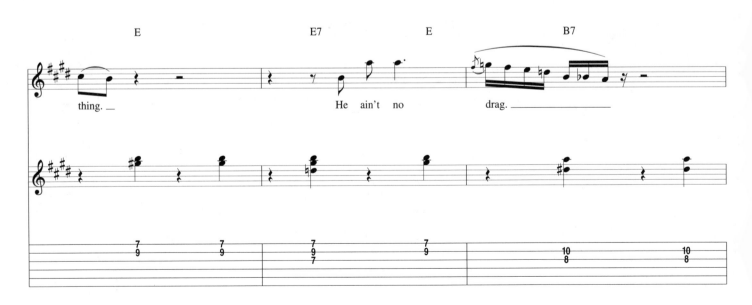

Shining Star

Words and Music by Maurice White, Philip Bailey and Larry Dunn

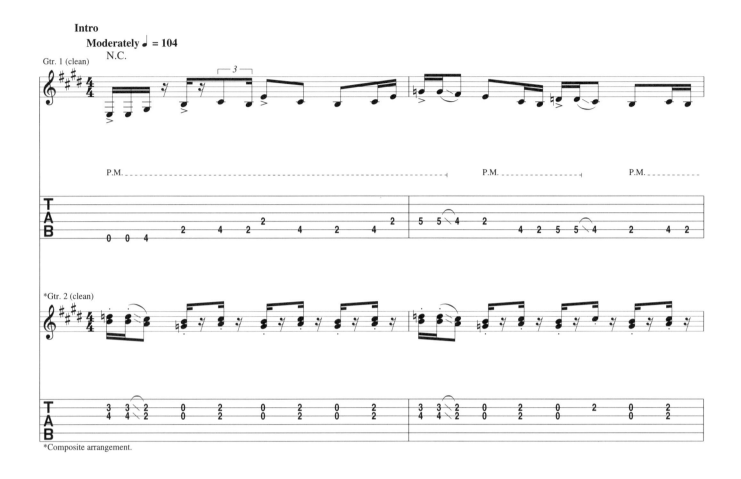

*Composite arrangement.

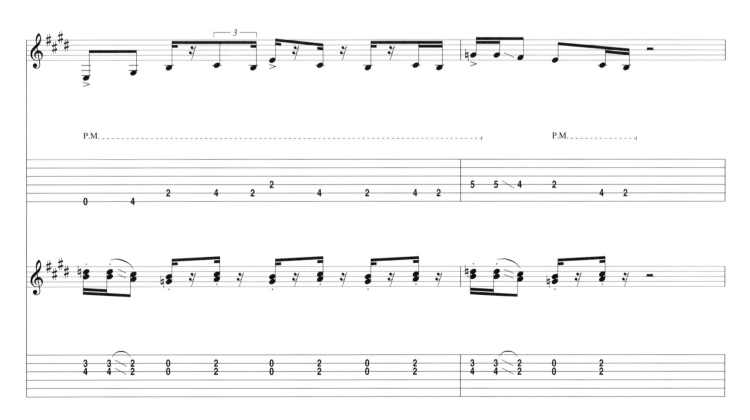

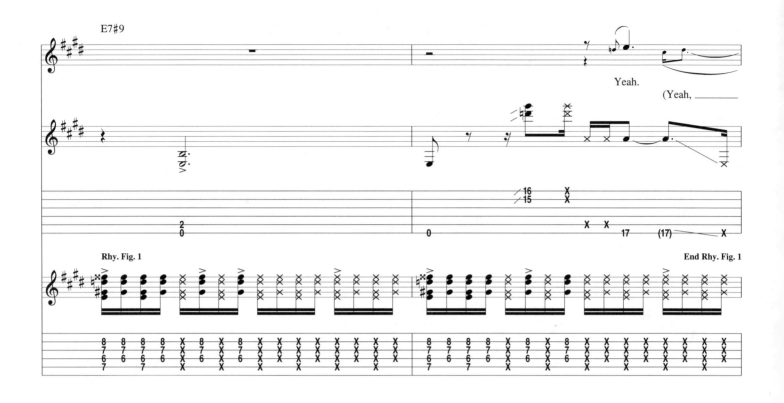

Yeah.

(Yeah,

Rhy. Fig. 1

End Rhy. Fig. 1

Gtr. 2: w/ Rhy. Fig. 1, simile

Hey.

Ha!

Gtr. 1

P.M. ----------- | P.M. ------------ | P.M. ----------------- | P.M. ----------- | P.M. ---

1/4

Verse

Gtr. 2: w/ Rhy. Fig. 1, 6 times, simile

E7#9

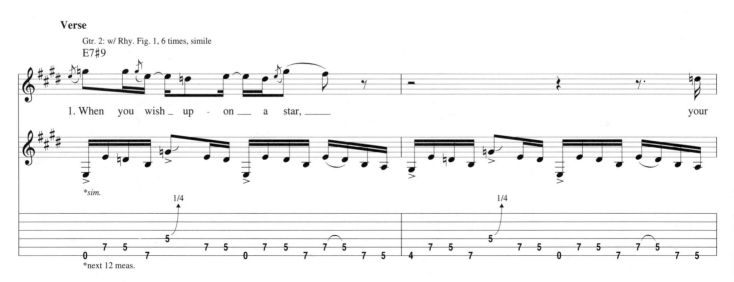

1. When you wish _ up - on _ a star, _____

your

*sim.

1/4

1/4

*next 12 meas.

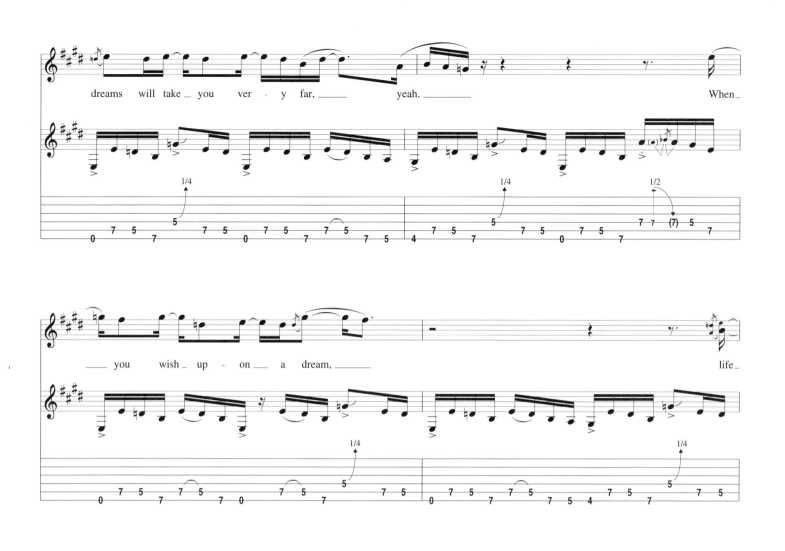

dreams will take __ you ver - y far, _____ yeah. _____ When_

__ you wish __ up - on __ a dream, _____ life_

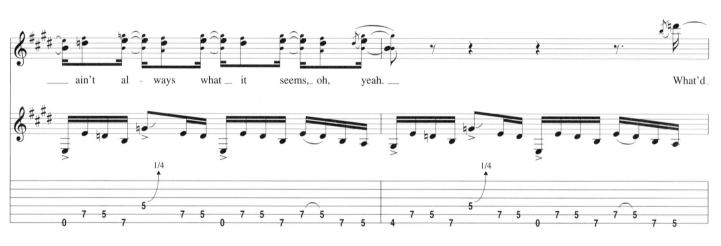

__ ain't al - ways what __ it seems, _ oh, yeah. __ What'd_

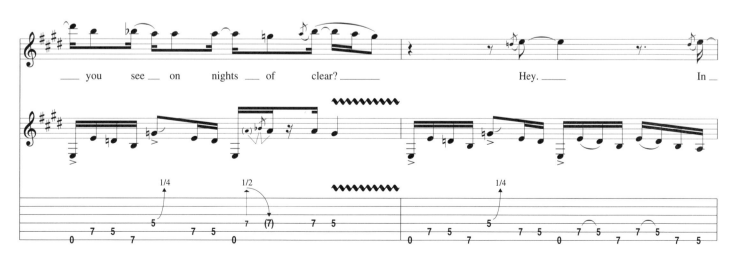

__ you see __ on nights __ of clear? _____ Hey. _____ In __

the sky — so ver - y dear, — yeah. — You're a

Chorus

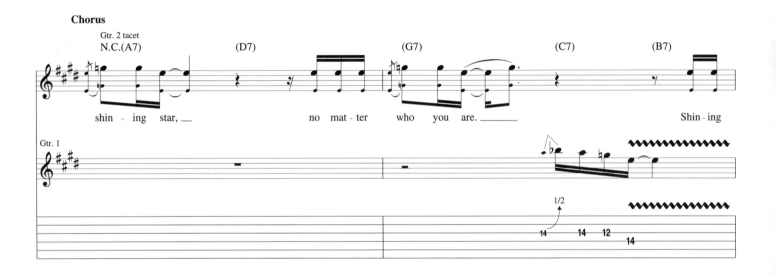

shin - ing star, — no mat - ter who you are. — Shin - ing

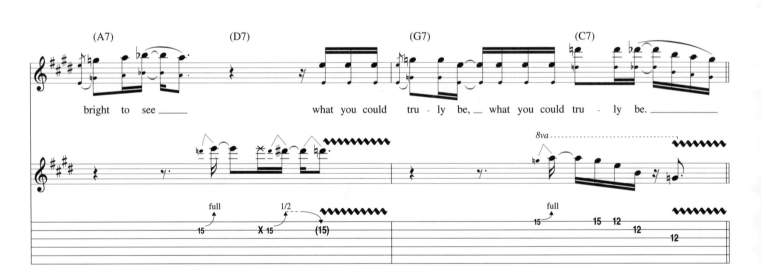

bright to see — what you could tru - ly be, — what you could tru - ly be. —

Interlude

Guitar Solo

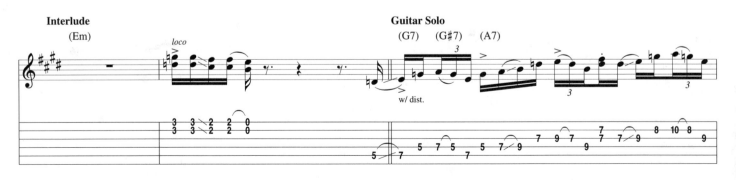

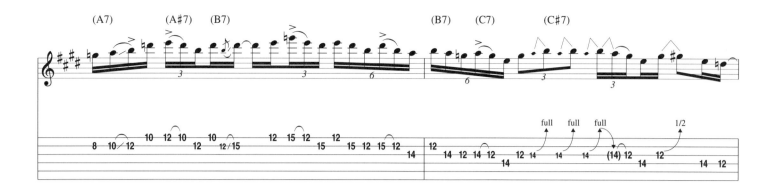

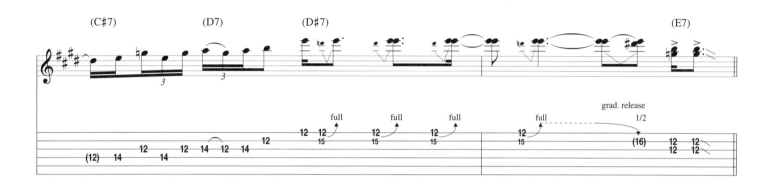

Verse

Gtr. 2: w/ Rhy. Fig. 1, 12 times, simile

(E7#9)

2. Shin - ing star _ comes in - to view, ____

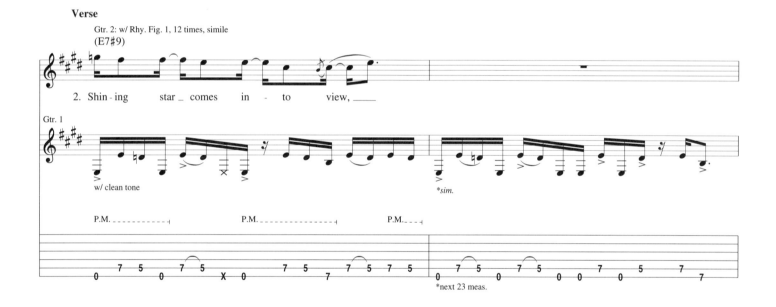

shine his watch - ful light _ on you. _ Yeah. ____ Give _

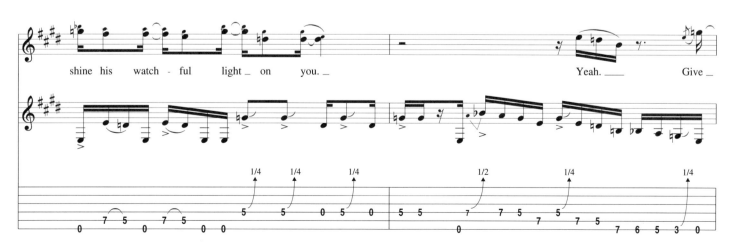

Shotgun

Words and Music by Autry DeWalt

*Key Signature denotes Ab Mixolydian.

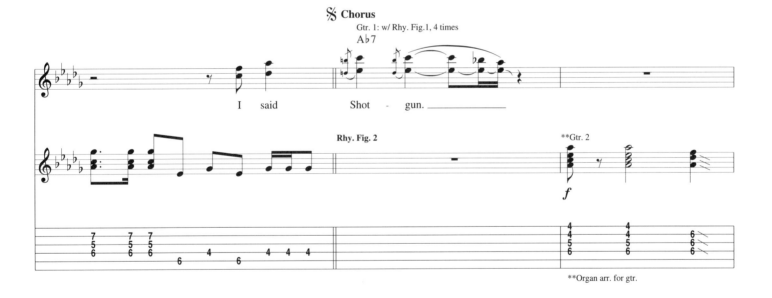

**Organ arr. for gtr.

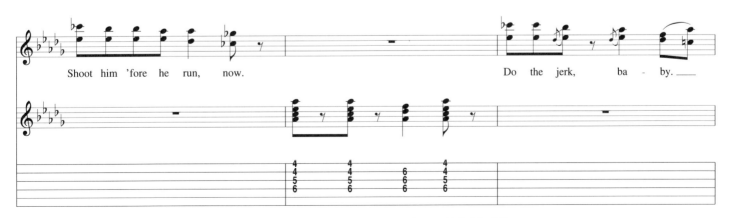

You Got the Love

Words and Music by Chaka Khan and Ray Parker

© Copyright 1974 by MCA MUSIC PUBLISHING, A Division of UNIVERSAL STUDIOS, INC.
International Copyright Secured   All Rights Reserved

MCA music publishing

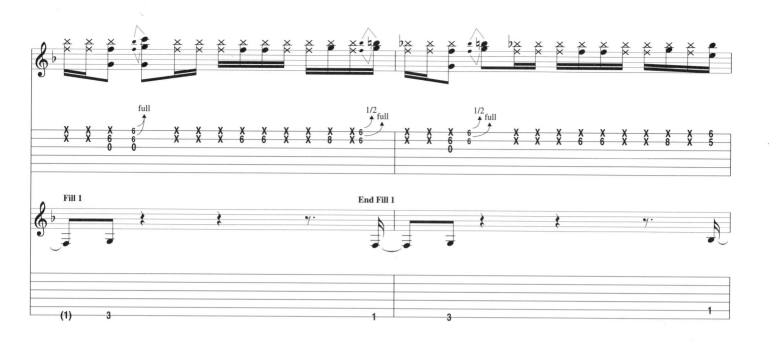

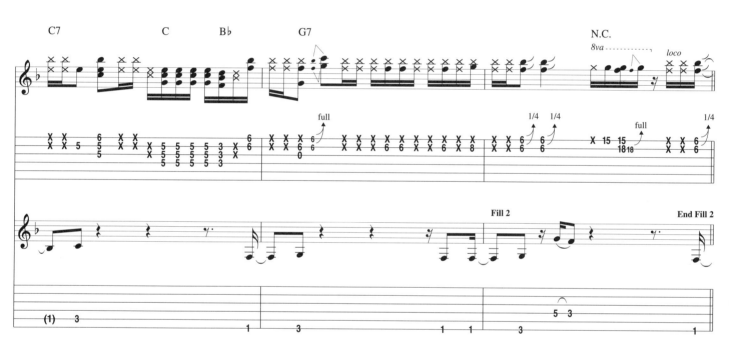

𝄉 Verse

Gtr. 2: w/ Riff A
Gtr. 1: w/ Rhy. Fig. 1, 2nd time, simile
Gtr. 4 tacet, 2nd time

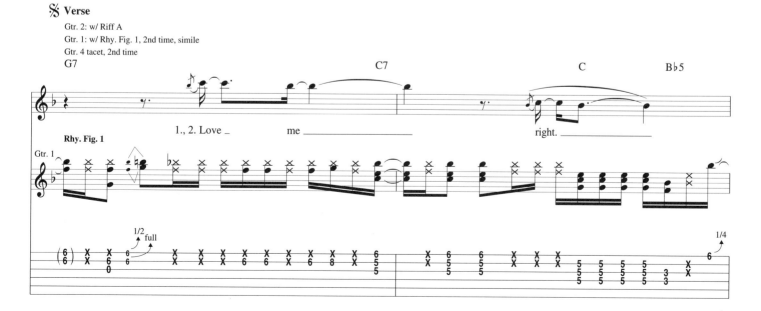

1., 2. Love _____ me _____ right. _____

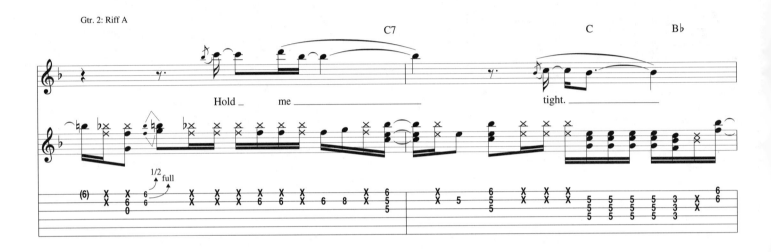

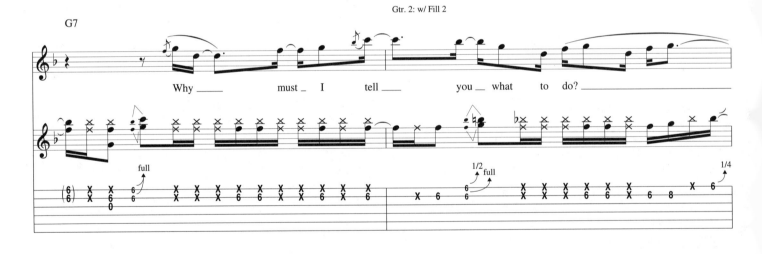

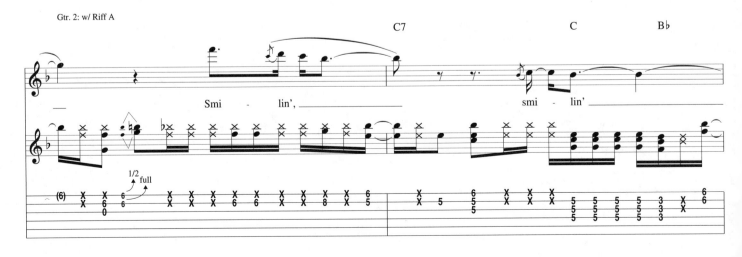

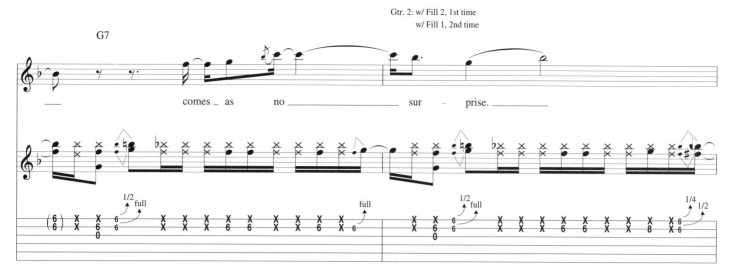

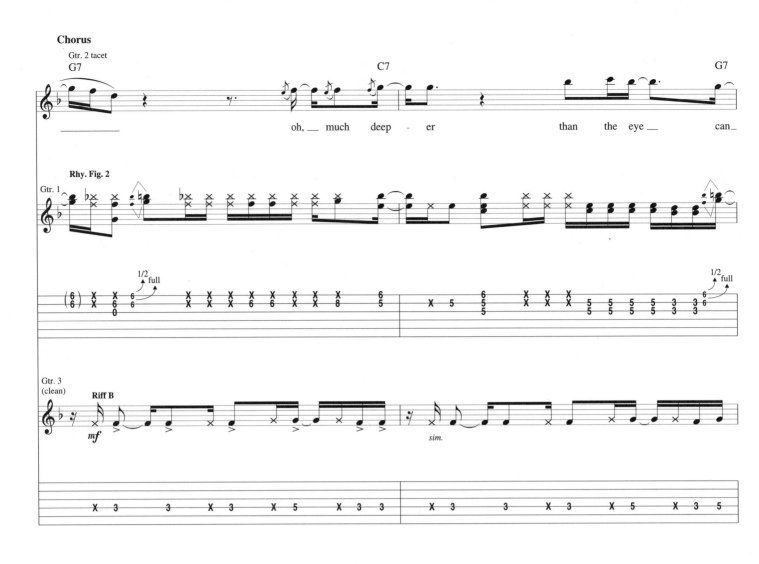

oh, __ much deep - er   than the eye __ can __

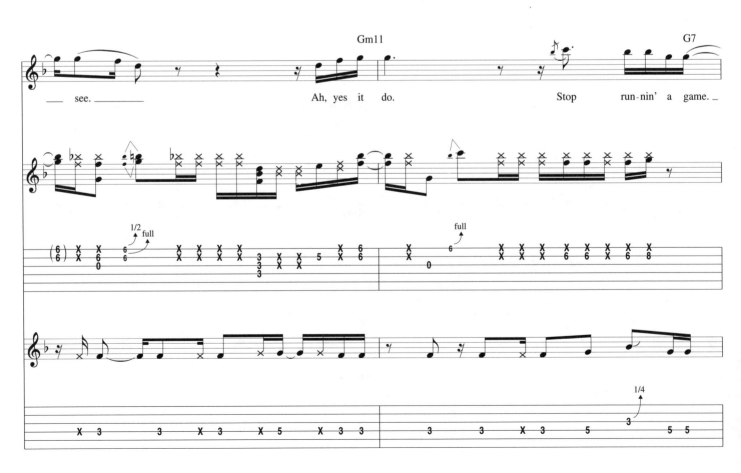

__ see. __   Ah, yes it do.   Stop run-nin' a game. __

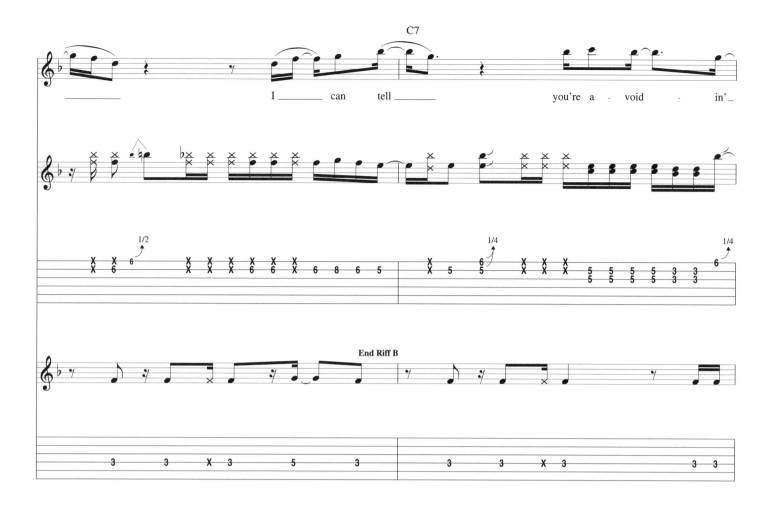

I ___ can tell ___ you're a - void - in' ___

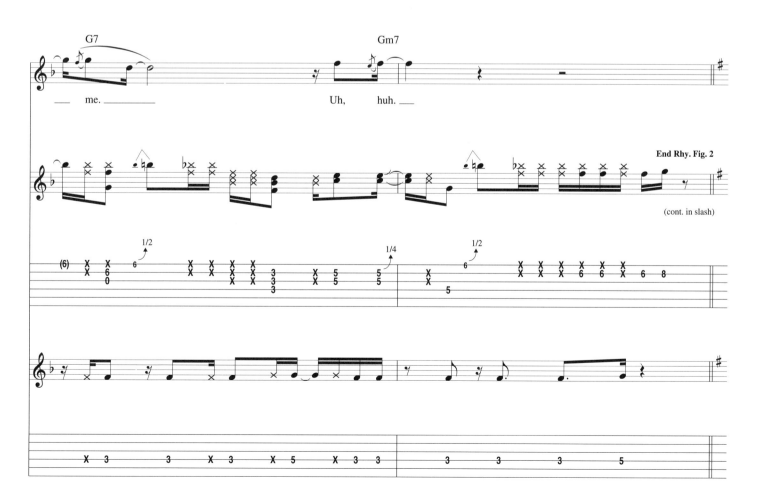

me. ___ Uh, huh. ___

(cont. in slash)

Bridge

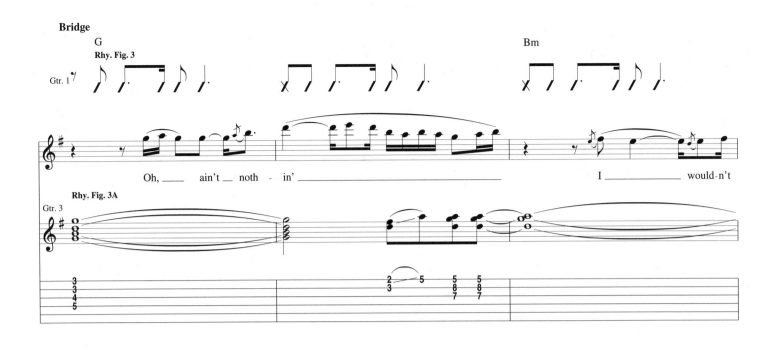

Oh, ___ ain't ___ noth - in' _____ I _____ would-n't

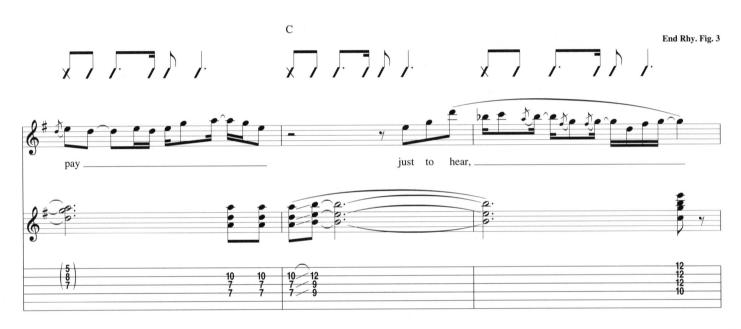

pay _____ just to hear, _____

Interlude

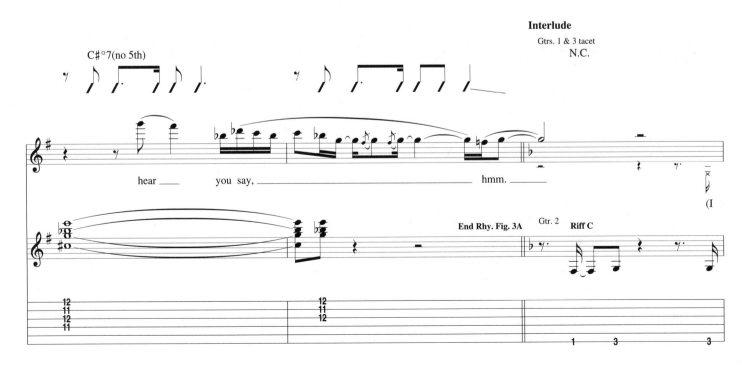

hear ____ you say, _____ hmm. _____

what you're giv - in', _____ mm, mm.

Bridge

Ain't __ noth - in' _____ I _____ would-n't pay,

oh, __ just to hear, _____ yeah, _____

just to hear _____ you say, _____ mm.

Interlude

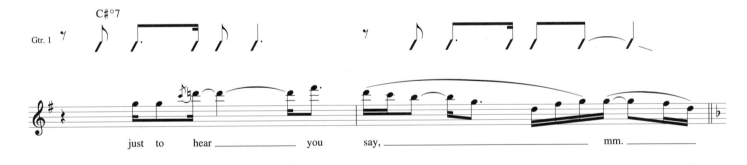

(I love ya'.

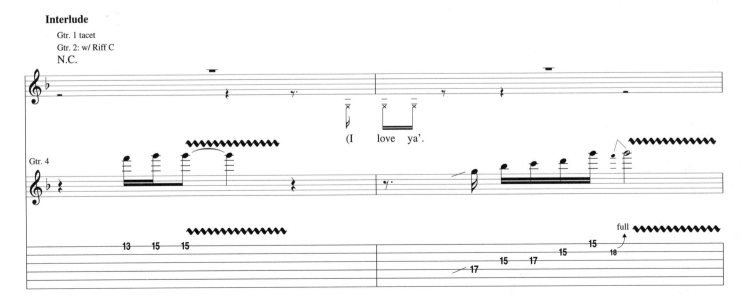

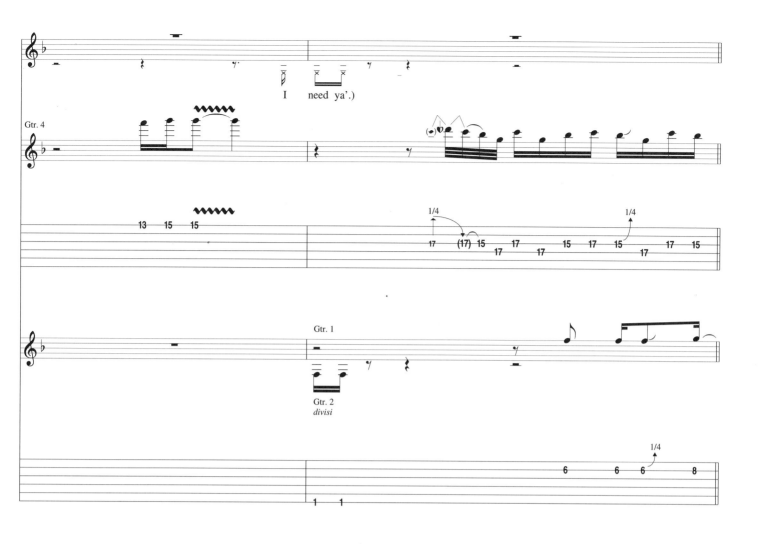

I need ya'.)

Gtr. 4

Gtr. 1

Gtr. 2
divisi

Guitar Solo

Gtr. 2 tacet
Gtr. 3: w/ Riff B, 1st 3 meas.
*G7
C7

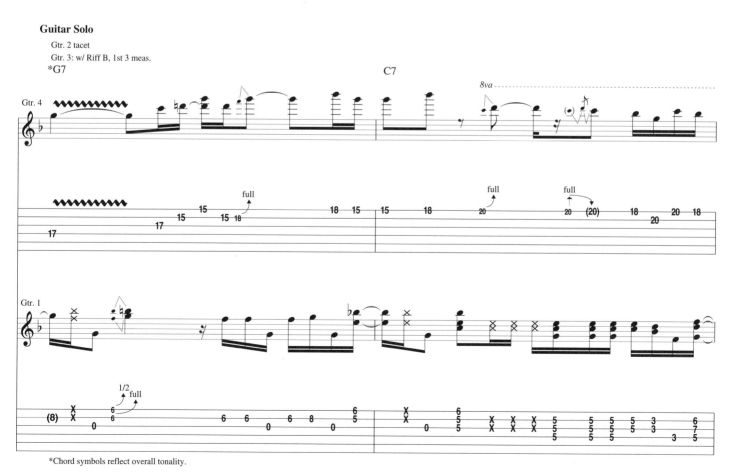

Gtr. 4

8va

Gtr. 1

*Chord symbols reflect overall tonality.

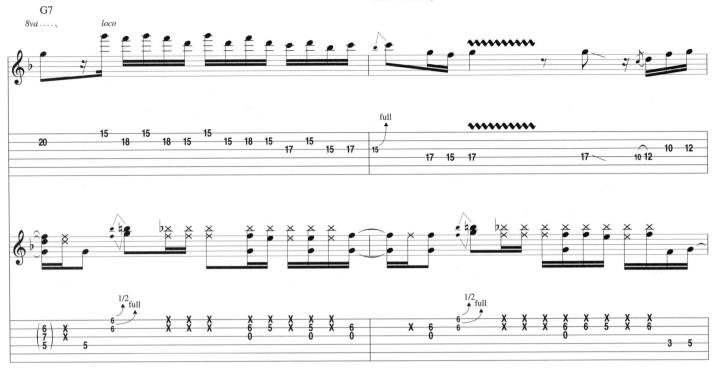

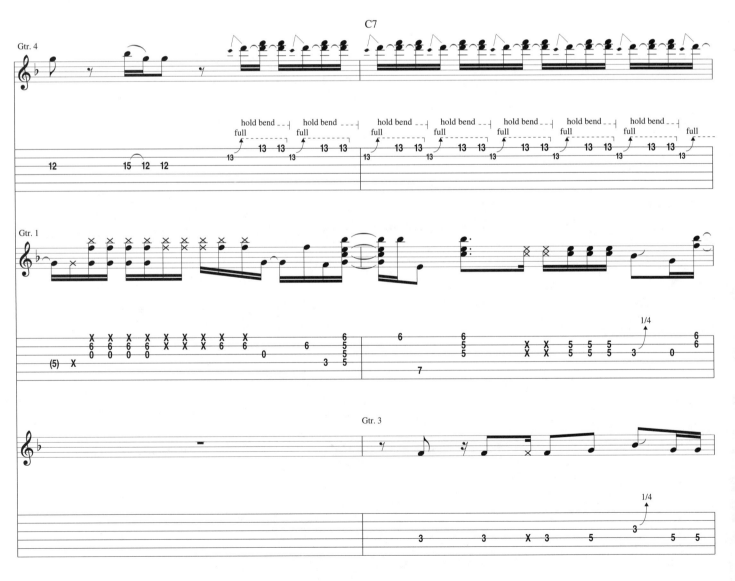

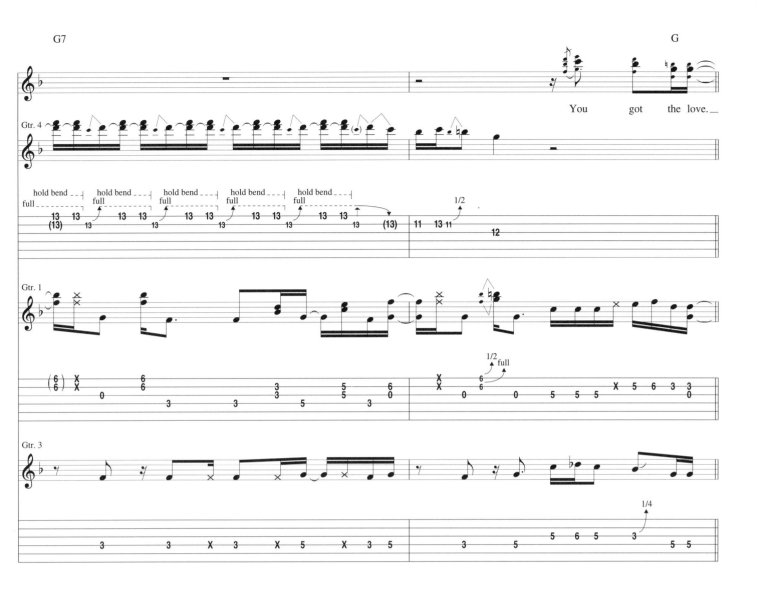

You got the love. __

Chorus

Gtr 3: w/ Riff B, 1st 3 meas.

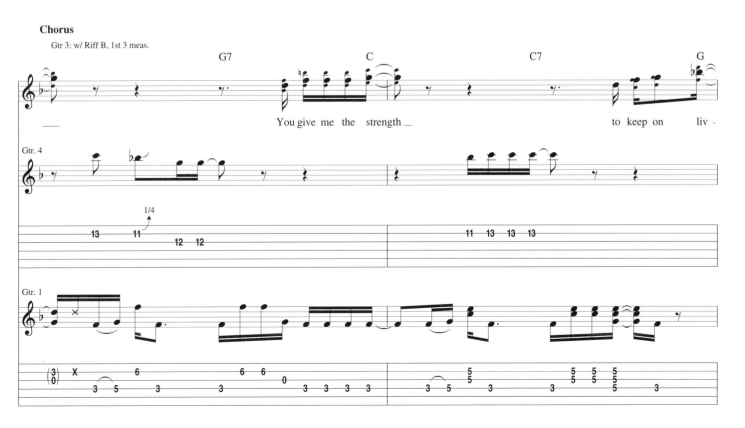

__ You give me the strength __ to keep on liv -

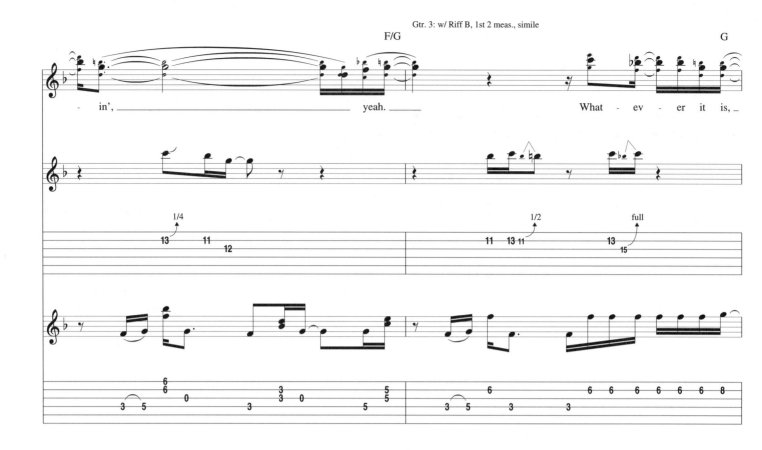

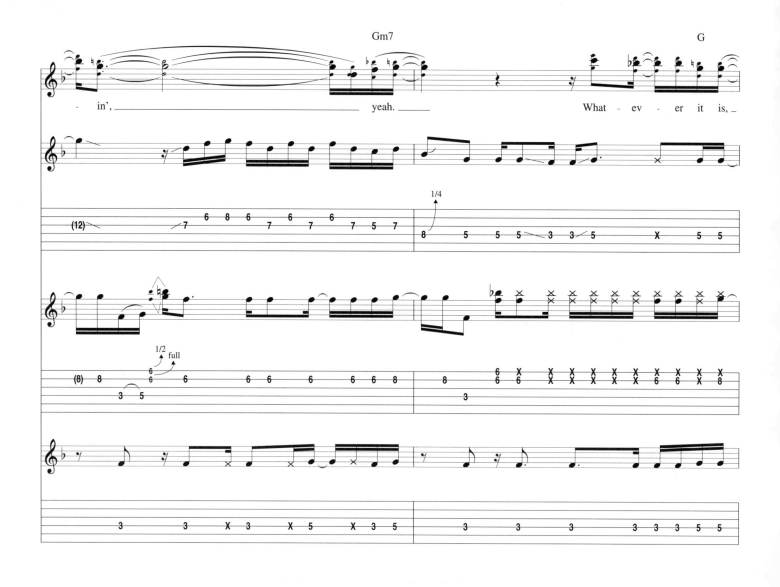

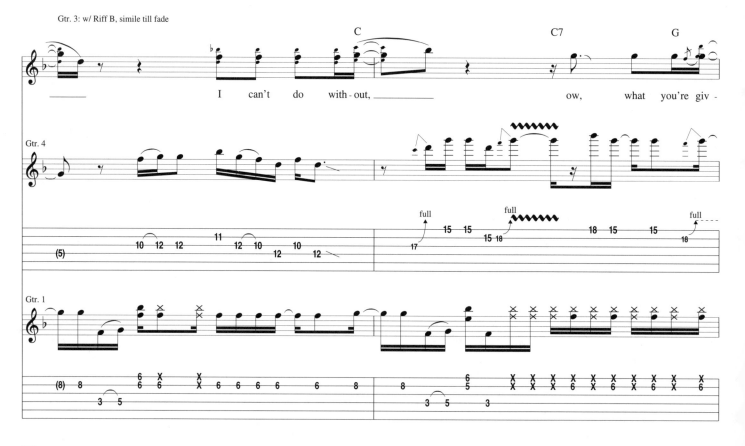

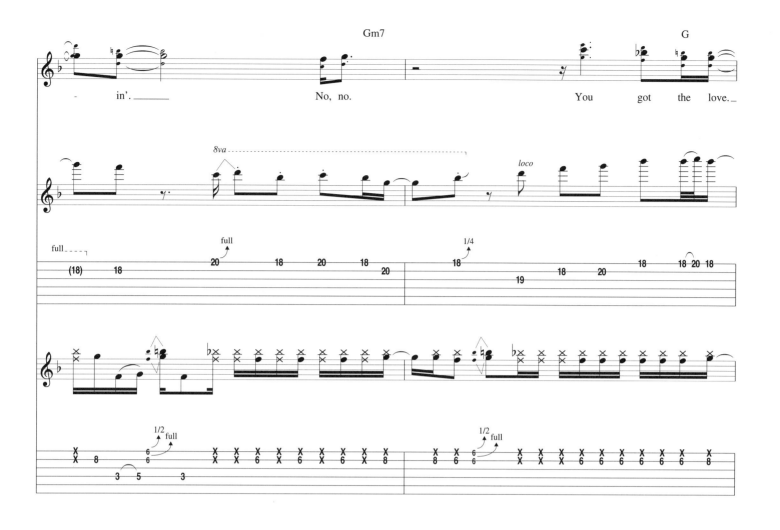

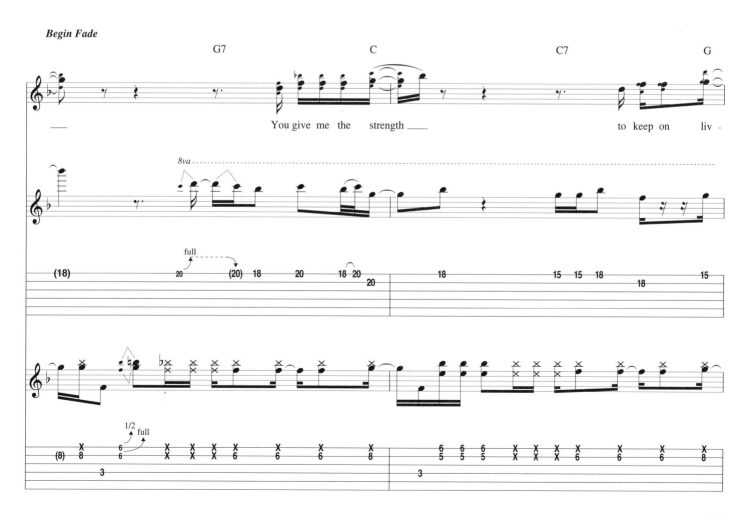

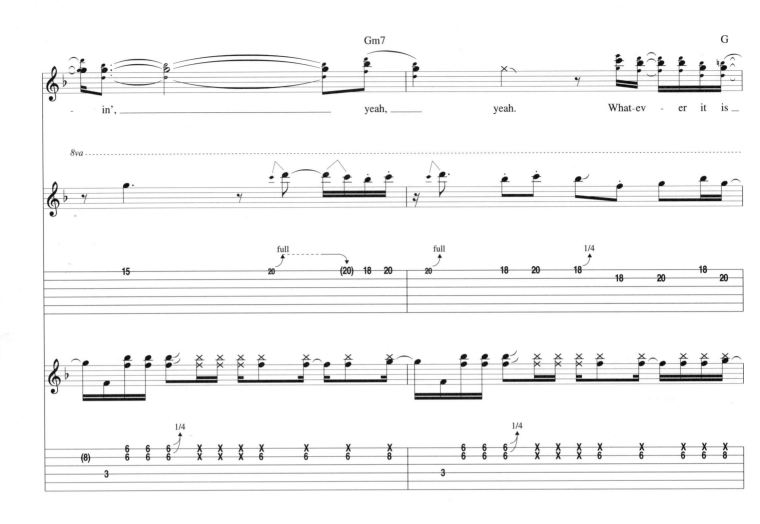

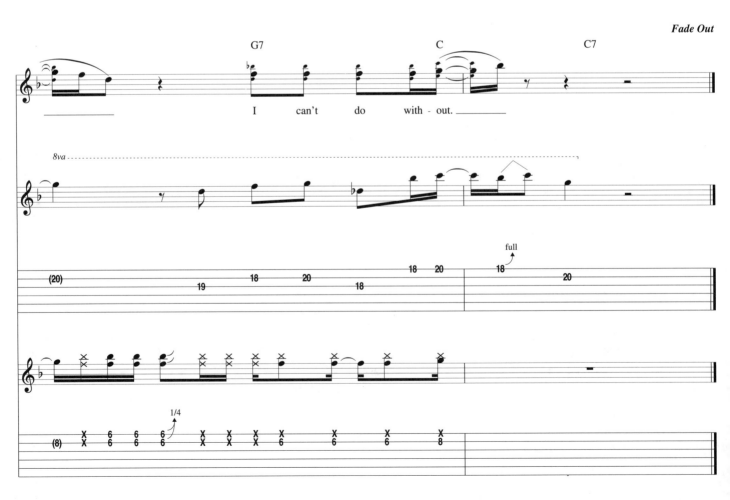

Guitar Notation Legend

Guitar Music can be notated three different ways: on a *musical staff*, in *tablature*, and in *rhythm slashes*.

RHYTHM SLASHES are written above the staff. Strum chords in the rhythm indicated. Use the chord diagrams found at the top of the first page of the transcription for the appropriate chord voicings. Round noteheads indicate single notes.

THE MUSICAL STAFF shows pitches and rhythms and is divided by bar lines into measures. Pitches are named after the first seven letters of the alphabet.

TABLATURE graphically represents the guitar fingerboard. Each horizontal line represents a string, and each number represents a fret.

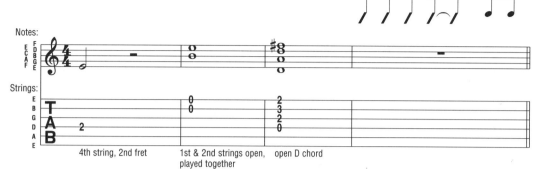

4th string, 2nd fret | 1st & 2nd strings open, played together | open D chord

HALF-STEP BEND: Strike the note and bend up 1/2 step.

WHOLE-STEP BEND: Strike the note and bend up one step.

GRACE NOTE BEND: Strike the note and bend up as indicated. The first note does not take up any time.

SLIGHT (MICROTONE) BEND: Strike the note and bend up 1/4 step.

BEND AND RELEASE: Strike the note and bend up as indicated, then release back to the original note. Only the first note is struck.

PRE-BEND: Bend the note as indicated, then strike it.

VIBRATO: The string is vibrated by rapidly bending and releasing the note with the fretting hand.

WIDE VIBRATO: The pitch is varied to a greater degree by vibrating with the fretting hand.

HAMMER-ON: Strike the first (lower) note with one finger, then sound the higher note (on the same string) with another finger by fretting it without picking.

PULL-OFF: Place both fingers on the notes to be sounded. Strike the first note and without picking, pull the finger off to sound the second (lower) note.

LEGATO SLIDE: Strike the first note and then slide the same fret-hand finger up or down to the second note. The second note is not struck.

SHIFT SLIDE: Same as legato slide, except the second note is struck.

TRILL: Very rapidly alternate between the notes indicated by continuously hammering on and pulling off.

TAPPING: Hammer ("tap") the fret indicated with the pick-hand index or middle finger and pull off to the note fretted by the fret hand.

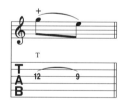

NATURAL HARMONIC: Strike the note while the fret-hand lightly touches the string directly over the fret indicated.

PINCH HARMONIC: The note is fretted normally and a harmonic is produced by adding the edge of the thumb or the tip of the index finger of the pick hand to the normal pick attack.

PICK SCRAPE: The edge of the pick is rubbed down (or up) the string, producing a scratchy sound.

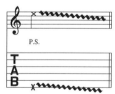

MUFFLED STRINGS: A percussive sound is produced by laying the fret hand across the string(s) without depressing, and striking them with the pick hand.

PALM MUTING: The note is partially muted by the pick hand lightly touching the string(s) just before the bridge.

RAKE: Drag the pick across the strings indicated with a single motion.

TREMOLO PICKING: The note is picked as rapidly and continuously as possible.

VIBRATO BAR DIVE AND RETURN: The pitch of the note or chord is dropped a specified number of steps (in rhythm) then returned to the original pitch.

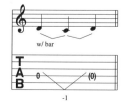

VIBRATO BAR SCOOP: Depress the bar just before striking the note, then quickly release the bar.

VIBRATO BAR DIP: Strike the note and then immediately drop a specified number of steps, then release back to the original pitch.